T5-BQA-593

Library of
Davidson College

FORMING MULTIMODAL TRANSPORTATION COMPANIES

A Conference Sponsored by the
American Enterprise Institute for Public Policy Research

FORMING MULTIMODAL TRANSPORTATION COMPANIES
BARRIERS, BENEFITS, AND PROBLEMS

A Conference Moderated by John W. Barnum

Edited by
Clinton H. Whitehurst, Jr.

American Enterprise Institute for Public Policy Research
Washington, D.C.

347.7
F 725

Library of Congress Cataloging in Publication Data

Main entry under title:

Forming multimodal transportation companies.

    (AEI symposia ; 79A)
    Proceedings of a conference sponsored by the
Institute, held in Washington, D.C., Feb. 1978.
    Bibliography: p. 171
    Includes index.
    1.   Carriers—United States—Congresses.
2.   Transportation—Law and legislation—United States—
Congresses.   3.   Corporation law—United States—
Congresses.   I.   Whitehurst, Clinton H., 1927–
II.   American Enterprise Institute for Public Policy Research.
III.   Series: American Enterprise Institute for Public
Policy Research. AEI symposia ; 79A.
KF1091.A75F67   346'.73'066   79-940
ISBN 0-8447-2147-6
ISBN 0-8447-2146-8 pbk.

AEI Symposia 79A

© 1978 by American Enterprise Institute for Public Policy Research,
Washington, D.C. All rights reserved. No part of this publication may be
used or reproduced in any manner whatsoever without permission in
writing from the American Enterprise Institute except in the case of
brief quotations embodied in news articles, critical articles, or reviews.

The views expressed in the publications of the American Enterprise Institute
are those of the authors and do not necessarily reflect the views of the staff,
advisory panels, officers, or trustees of AEI. *79-5864*

"American Enterprise Institute" is the registered service mark of the
American Enterprise Institute for Public Policy Research.

Printed in the United States of America

The American Enterprise Institute for Public Policy Research, established in 1943, is a publicly supported, nonpartisan, research and educational organization. Its purpose is to assist policy makers, scholars, businessmen, the press, and the public by providing objective analysis of national and international issues. Views expressed in the institute's publications are those of the authors and do not necessarily reflect the views of the staff, advisory panels, officers, or trustees of AEI.

Council of Academic Advisers

Paul W. McCracken, *Chairman, Edmund Ezra Day University Professor of Business Administration, University of Michigan*

Robert H. Bork, *Alexander M. Bickel Professor of Public Law, Yale Law School*

Kenneth W. Dam, *Harold J. and Marion F. Green Professor of Law, University of Chicago Law School*

Donald C. Hellmann, *Professor of Political Science and International Studies, University of Washington*

D. Gale Johnson, *Eliakim Hastings Moore Distinguished Service Professor of Economics and Provost, University of Chicago*

Robert A. Nisbet, *Resident Scholar, American Enterprise Institute*

Herbert Stein, *A. Willis Robertson Professor of Economics, University of Virginia*

Marina v. N. Whitman, *Distinguished Public Service Professor of Economics, University of Pittsburgh*

James Q. Wilson, *Henry Lee Shattuck Professor of Government, Harvard University*

Executive Committee

Herman J. Schmidt, *Chairman of the Board*

William J. Baroody, Jr., *President*

Charles T. Fisher III, *Treasurer*

Richard J. Farrell

Richard B. Madden

Richard D. Wood

Gary L. Jones, *Vice President, Administration*

Edward Styles, *Director of Publications*

Program Directors

Russell Chapin, *Legislative Analyses*

Robert B. Helms, *Health Policy Studies*

Thomas F. Johnson, *Economic Policy Studies*

Sidney L. Jones, *Seminar Programs*

Marvin H. Kosters/James C. Miller III, *Government Regulation Studies*

Jack Meyer, *Special Projects (acting)*

W. S. Moore, *Legal Policy Studies*

Rudolph G. Penner, *Tax Policy Studies*

Howard R. Penniman/Austin Ranney, *Political and Social Processes*

Robert J. Pranger, *Foreign and Defense Policy Studies*

Periodicals

AEI Economist, Herbert Stein, Editor

AEI Foreign Policy and Defense Review, Robert J. Pranger and Donald C. Hellmann, Co-Editors

Public Opinion, Seymour Martin Lipset, Ben J. Wattenberg, Co-Editors; David R. Gergen, Managing Editor

Regulation, Antonin Scalia and Murray L. Weidenbaum, Co-Editors; Anne Brunsdale, Managing Editor

William J. Baroody, Sr., *Counsellor and Chairman, Development Committee*

PARTICIPANTS

Brock Adams
Secretary of Transportation

Thomas G. Allison
Counsel, Senate Committee on Appropriations
Former Chief Counsel, Senate Committee on Commerce

W. J. Amoss
President
Lykes Bros. Steamship Co., Inc.

John W. Barnum
Resident Fellow, American Enterprise Institute, and
Former Deputy Secretary, U.S. Department of Transportation

B. F. Biaggini
Chairman and Chief Executive
Southern Pacific Transportation Co.

Thomas W. Browne
Vice President
United Parcel Service

J. Joseph Cotter
Administrative Assistant to the
General President
International Brotherhood of Teamsters, Chauffeurs,
Warehousemen & Helpers of America

William T. Druhan
Staff Director
House Subcommittee on Transportation and Commerce

Robert C. Dryden
Vice President, Traffic
Georgia Highway Express, Inc.

Rodney E. Eyster
Consultant, American Enterprise Institute
Former General Counsel, U.S. Department of Transportation

Richard Fishbein
Managing Director
Lehman Brothers Kuhn Loeb Incorporated

Frank E. Fitzsimmons
General President
International Brotherhood of Teamsters, Chauffeurs,
Warehousemen & Helpers of America

Paul Hall
President, Seafarers International Union of North America, and
President, Maritime Trades Department, AFL-CIO

J. Robert Hard
Vice President
American Commercial Barge Line Company

Charles I. Hiltzheimer
Chairman and Chief Executive Officer
Sea-Land Service, Inc.

Vernon T. Jones
President
Williams Pipe Line Company

Alfred E. Kahn
Chairman
Civil Aeronautics Board

Linda Kamm
General Counsel
U.S. Department of Transportation

Anthony B. Low-Beer
L. F. Rothschild, Unterberg, Towbin

Kenneth McLaughlin
President
Universal Carloading & Distributing Co., Inc.

William G. Mahoney
Highsaw, Mahoney & Friedman

David M. Munro
Second Vice President
John Hancock Mutual Life Insurance Company

A. Daniel O'Neal, Jr.
Chairman
Interstate Commerce Commission

Jack Pearce
Pearce & Brand

Paul O. Roberts
Director, Center for Transportation Studies
Massachusetts Institute of Technology

Harvey M. Romoff
Assistant Vice President, Corporate Development
Canadian Pacific

Fred B. Rooney
Chairman
House Subcommittee on Transportation and Commerce

A. Robert Schaefer
Director of Marketing
Emery Distribution Systems Inc.

Elliott M. Seiden
Chief, Transportation Section
Antitrust Division
U.S. Department of Justice

Harold M. Shay
President
Shay's Service Inc.

Bud Shuster
Ranking Minority Member
House Subcommittee on Surface Transportation

William Jarrel Smith, Jr.
Deputy Managing Director
Federal Maritime Commission

William K. Smith
Vice President
General Mills, Inc.

James V. Springrose
Vice President, Transportation
Cargill Incorporated

John J. Terry
Group Vice President, Land Transportation
IU International Management Corporation

Hays T. Watkins
Chairman and President
Chessie System, Inc.

Clinton H. Whitehurst, Jr.
Clemson University

Dillon Winship, Jr.
President, Georgia Highway Express, Inc., and
Former Chairman, American Trucking Associations

Clifford L. Worth
General Traffic Manager
Westvaco Company

———————◆———————

Colonel William Crabbe, Industrial College of the Armed Forces

David J. DeBoer, Chief, Transportation Policy Planning, Rail Services Planning Office, Interstate Commerce Commission

William J. Dempsey, President, Association of American Railroads

Peter J. Finnerty, Vice President, Public Affairs, Sea-Land Service, Inc.

Daniel V. Flanagan, Government Affairs Representative, Southern Pacific Company

John F. Fryer, Assistant Counsel, House Committee on Public Works and Transportation

Edwin K. Hall, General Counsel, Senate Committee on Commerce, Science and Transportation

Edward R. Hamburger, General Counsel, National Transportation Policy Study Commission

Christopher Hart, Special Assistant to the General Counsel, U.S. Department of Transportation

Thomas F. Johnson, Director, Economic Policy Studies, American Enterprise Institute

Edward V. Kiley, Vice President, American Trucking Associations, Inc.

Marvin H. Kosters, Director, Center for the Study of Government Regulation, American Enterprise Institute

Edward LeMieux, Special Assistant to the Commanding General, Military Traffic Management Command

Kevin McCarthy, Assistant to Congressman Rooney

James C. Miller III, Co-director, Center for the Study of Government Regulation, American Enterprise Institute

J. Paul Molloy, Associate Counsel, House Committee on Interstate and Foreign Commerce

Larry Reida, Minority Counsel, House Committee on Public Works and Transportation

Marshall Sage, Administrative Assistant to the National Legislative Director, United Transportation Union

Richard Shreve, Cargo Services Department, Air Transport Association of America

Elwin W. Sill, Industrial College of the Armed Forces

John W. Snow, Vice President, Chessie System, Inc.

William R. Southard, Assistant to the Director, Bureau of Economics, Interstate Commerce Commission

Douglas W. Svendson, Counsel, Senate Committee on Surface Transportation

John E. Wild, Executive Director, National Transportation Policy Study Commission

CONTENTS

FOREWORD

John W. Barnum

"Common ownership is cannibalistic," says a former chairman of the American Trucking Associations. "It will not create intermodalism." The biggest problem for the common carrier transportation industry, as he sees it, is not the barriers to multimodal ownership but private carriage.

The chairman of the Southern Pacific, however, suggests that the biggest problem for all common carriers is too much regulation. "The people sitting around this table who are pretty well satisfied with their situation right now will be asking Congress for more protection ten or fifteen years from now." He adds, "I am all for common ownership and would be supportive of any change in the laws that would make it easier for multimodal transportation companies to develop."

"Are we perhaps tilting at windmills that are not even there?" asks a barge line vice president who thinks that the statutory barriers are minimal. We are tilting at windmills if we talk about the "overwhelming power of multimodal giants," argues the chief executive of the Chessie System.

It's a "ho-hum, so-what?" kind of subject to a major shipper. "The probability that [multimodal ownership] would improve the current bulk distribution system is very doubtful," says another major shipper. A third shipper identifies specific benefits he would enjoy if he could deal with multimodal carriers: simplicity; better service, equipment, and pricing; and easier settlement of damage claims. The shippers' collective view is that the danger of more regulation to protect the single-mode company and the disadvantages of dealing with monolithic institutions are more ominous than the danger of monopolies as such.

A railroad labor spokesman believes that adoption of multimodal operations would result in elimination of branch and secondary main lines—though a railroad chief executive disagrees. The labor spokesman believes that multimodalism should increase rail employee productivity, but he predicts that it would also result in a net loss of employment, as well as uncertainty and morale problems among em-

1

ployees. Any statutory or regulatory move toward multimodal operations, he argues, must protect the individual employees and provide
safeguards against disruption of the existing separate representation of
railroad and trucking employees.

A Teamster official, expressing concern for the health of surface
transportation and many recent trucking company bankruptcies and
rail insolvencies, says that the basic problem has been the government's insistence on cheap rates and redundant services. A railroad
executive observes that it is the shippers who like the flexibility of
being able to play one mode against the other and who might fear
that integrated companies would reduce that flexibility.

The Seafarers' president believes that "multimodal ownership
is a logical evolution for the transportation network [and] is likely to
lead to greater efficiencies in transportation." More important from his
vantage point, it would integrate marine transportation into the total
network for the first time. "Labor can support any such evolution."

"The formation of multimodal companies is likely to have a favorable effect on carriers' ability to obtain financing [because it would]
lead to financially stronger enterprises irrespective of any operating
economies of multimodal operation," says an investment banker. A
railroad securities analyst is concerned, however, that capital available
to a transportation conglomerate would be diverted to the more profitable elements—the truck and barge operations.

A trucking executive expresses concern that he might find himself competing with a truck line owned by a railroad that is subsidized
by the federal government. He is all for regulatory changes that help
the railroads stay alive, but in his European trucking operations he
has already experienced the disadvantages of competing with govern-
ment-subsidized transportation companies.

The deputy managing director of the Federal Maritime Commission points out that all U.S.-flag companies compete internationally
with integrated transportation companies, all of which are free to
come into the liner trades to the United States. Airfreight and trucking experts echo the concern for having to compete with integrated
foreign competition. An ocean freight chief executive suggests that
obtaining authority for through-rate making—ocean and rail—could
benefit the shippers more than multimodal ownership.

A Canadian Pacific executive believes, on the basis of his experience in Canada where there are multimodal companies, that rate
regulation—or deregulation—is a more significant spur to intermodalism and efficient transportation than multimodal ownership.

A transportation economist suggests that the key to successful
multimodal operations is the relationship between length of haul and
traffic density. To him the problem is the thinness of the markets, but

2

the opportunities are substantial. A trucking executive looking at the same data concludes that multimodal ownership will not help railroads because they are more likely to increase their intermodal (that is, piggyback) freight by catering to all truckers, private and for-hire, rather than by acquiring any one motor carrier. In the same vein, another trucking president sees "no way for a single entity to take over the local and short-haul carrier, which is the guts of a transportation system that takes care of rural and urban America." He also believes that common ownership would deter intermodalism and be harmful to the shipping public.

The secretary of transportation does not have any doubts: "I think that removing the barriers to intermodal transportation systems, be they regulatory or otherwise, is absolutely necessary." The chairman of the Civil Aeronautics Board (CAB) concludes that the flat prohibition of integration does not make sense since integration is not generally prohibited in the economy. He feels that the burden of proof should be on those who argue that intermodal ownership is bad. The chairman notes that the CAB had found that the integrated air and surface freight forwarders have not overwhelmed the independent, single-mode forwarders, but rather have stimulated competition and brought service to additional markets. He and the general counsel of the Department of Transportation agree, however, that we should be mindful of discriminatory treatment that gives integrated companies unequal access to the market, although a greater market share may also result from the efficiency advantages of integration.

The Antitrust Division says the existing transportation statutes on *intra*modal mergers plus its traditional Clayton Act Section 7 antitrust analysis are adequate to address both the horizontal and the vertical aspects of intermodal ownership either by acquisition or by internal expansion. And the Antitrust Division, like the CAB chairman, would in any event like to eliminate the test of public convenience and necessity.

After a day of debate among forty transportation industry and labor executives, shippers, financiers, and government transportation officials, there was not any consensus on barriers to multimodal ownership except that they are not the most important problem in transportation. Yet, as one shipper who was not sure of the benefits said, "We should not deny the chance to develop those opportunities. I don't think we can restrict the ingenuity of man, and if someone wants to develop multimodal ownership, he should be allowed to do so." The issue may not be paramount and the potential gains not great, observed another, but most progress is made by little steps, and any incremental gains would be worth having.

FOREWORD

It was agreed that progress in transportation can be made only by thoughtful exploration of the advantages and disadvantages of a proposal, by the exchange of views among the interested elements of the transportation community, and by frank recognition of the political problems inherent in any change. That was the purpose of this conference and of this volume.

INTRODUCTION

Clinton H. Whitehurst, Jr.

In 1967 an article in *U.S. News and World Report* entitled "Trucks, Trains, Planes, Boats, All in One Company?" reviewed the case for removing institutional barriers to permit common ownership of different transport modes. What has happened in the ten years since? While it would be an exaggeration to assert that amending the law to allow formation of multimodal transportation companies is a "front burner" issue in 1978, it is nonetheless one of continuing interest within the transportation industry and academic community. (See the annotated bibliography in this volume, and note the diversity of the authors, reports, and publications.)

In recent years, deregulation of transportation has received a significant share of presidential, congressional, academic, industry, and public attention. In 1975 President Ford submitted proposals to Congress to deregulate rail, air, and truck transport. The Railroad Revitalization and Regulatory Reform Act of 1976, the so-called 4R legislation, contained some measure of regulatory reform. And in 1978, with the endorsement of the Carter administration, an airline deregulation bill went before Congress, while hearings on trucking deregulation continued. On another front, it seemed likely that for the first time in history user fees (taxes) would be collected from inland waterway users. This proposal, which received the endorsement of President Carter and former President Ford, was designed as much to achieve equity between modes as to raise revenues for waterway improvements, operation, and maintenance.

Other important factors in the overall transportation environment are: (1) the need to achieve efficient energy use in transportation; (2) the growing public expenditure necessary to provide a viable transportation system (since 1974 federal expenditures have increased by approximately $6 billion in this respect); and (3) the precarious financial health of some segments of the transportation industry. The financial plight of the northeastern and some midwestern railroads is a matter of record; in addition, the operating subsidy for the merchant marine is approaching $500 million annually, and in 1977 the rate of

5

return on investment for many airlines (including cargo carriers) was inadequate to fund the necessary replacement of their fleets over the next fifteen years.

In this context the American Enterprise Institute deemed it appropriate to sponsor a conference on whether it would be in the nation's best interest to eliminate barriers to the formation of multimodal transportation companies. Important questions considered were: How would carriers react to the elimination of statutory and regulatory barriers to multimodal ownership? How would the formation of multimodal companies affect transportation labor? How would it affect shippers? Would multimodal firms be financially stronger—able to attract private capital more easily and concomitantly to be less dependent on government? If multimodal firms came into being, how would they be regulated? How would a competitive environment be maintained? Would they offer better and cheaper service to the shipper? Do shippers perceive the need for "one-stop shopping" in arranging their transportation requirements? What are the views of the present regulatory agencies (Civil Aeronautics Board, Federal Maritime Commission, and Interstate Commerce Commission) as well as the Department of Justice? Related issues include: Would multimodal firms, in fact, be more energy efficient? Would removing legal barriers to common ownership be simply another step in the deregulation process already begun? Are present regulatory impediments to the formation of multimodal firms inequitable with respect to the different modes?

To consider these as well as other questions, a group of distinguished participants, representing every transportation interest—carriers, shippers, the financial community, labor, and relevant congressional committees and government agencies—met on February 23, 1978, in a one-day conference to debate the issue of multimodal transportation companies. Prior to the conference, each participant was furnished a set of three background papers prepared by well-known authorities familiar with the subject:

- Rodney E. Eyster, a 1957 Yale Law School graduate, served as general counsel for the Department of Transportation from December 1973 to June 1975. Mr. Eyster is a member of the bar in New York, Connecticut, and Illinois and at present resides in Washington, D.C.

- Paul O. Roberts received his Ph.D. from Northwestern University in 1966, served as director of the Center for Transportation Studies at the Massachusetts Institute of Technology from 1972 to 1978, and is now professor of transportation at that institution. He is the author of numerous books and articles in the field of transportation.

- Harvey M. Romoff, a 1957 graduate of McGill University and postgraduate fellow at the Massachusetts Institute of Technology, joined Canadian Pacific as a research economist in 1960. At present he is assistant vice president for corporate development, Canadian Pacific Limited.

The background papers by these men provided an in-depth review and analysis of three topics: the present law, the economics of multimodal ownership, and the Canadian experience with multimodal transportation companies. The conference debate was lively, informed, and at times humorous. To capture the views of participants faithfully, extreme care has been used in editing. Remarks, impromptu discussion, and informal comments are in sequence and entirely in context.

The proceedings are arranged in two parts. Part I includes the three background papers; Part II is the conference discussion and the luncheon address of Secretary of Transportation Brock Adams. An annotated bibliography of publications on multimodal transportation companies is appended. In their entirety, the proceedings provide an authoritative and current reference document on the issue of multimodal transportation companies. It should prove of value to transportation practitioners and scholars alike.

PART
ONE
PAPERS

Federal Rules on Intermodal Ownership of Common Carriers

Rodney E. Eyster

A simplified guide to federal rules on intermodal ownership of common carriers is presented in an appendix table, page 19. The rules to which the table refers are those which apply solely because ownership of two or more different modes would result from a particular transaction or new service. These special rules for multimodal ownership are in addition to the general rules of the Interstate Commerce Act (ICA), applicable in the absence of intermodal considerations, that mergers and other acquisitions involving two or more carriers must be consistent with the public interest (ICA § 5(2)(b)). The rules indicated in the table do not attempt to take account of modal characteristics that might be relevant to ordinary tests, such as being fit or able.

Both points are important and may be simply illustrated. If a motor carrier applies for a water carrier certificate, it must prove itself "fit, willing, and able" and must establish "public convenience and necessity" (ICA § 309(c)). If it seeks operating authority as an air forwarder, it must make the same showings (Federal Aviation Act [FAAct] § 408(b)) *and* convince the Civil Aeronautics Board (CAB) that its entry into air forwarding would be good for air commerce. The characteristics of the motor carrier—its routes, territories, services, commodities—would be paramount in determining the success of its application.[1] The table does not attempt to characterize the myriad ways those characteristics might affect whether the motor carrier would, for example, be deemed financially fit.

The above examples also serve to illustrate what appears to be an anomaly. Why do the motor carrier's routes concern the CAB as to possible effects on air commerce and not concern the ICC as to water commerce? There are two answers. One is historical accident. When special rules for ownership of water carriers were written into the Panama Canal Act of 1912 (37 Stat. 560, 566-67), motor carriers were not federally regulated and, more important, nobody worried about their economic power to engage in predatory practices. The

---

[1] The applicant's surface authorities must be extensive enough to have the potential of stimulating air commerce, but not so extensive as to pose a threat to existing air carriers and forwarders. See appendix table, note H.

other answer is that the Interstate Commerce Commission (ICC) probably would be concerned about the relation between the territories and routes served by the motor and water carriers. The omission from the table indicates only that the Congress has not provided specially for motor-water ownerships, and the ICC has not said how it would interpret its general authority in that type of case. In the converse situation, after a special requirement for water carrier–motor carrier operations was removed by Congress, the ICC found other ways to protect competing motor carriers.[2] Further, in the rail-water cases the ICC has consistently said its main concern is preservation of competition on the water.[3]

Thus it may be said, generally, that when agency approval is required—whether by a specific authority to grant an exception or by a general requirement, such as a certificate—the anomalies created by Congress tend to disappear.

Another generalization is that the rules applicable to acquisition of ownership are equally applicable to acquisition of control by lease, management contract, or otherwise and to joint operations. The same rules generally apply to authorization for establishing a new carrier or a new service using another mode. Generally the prohibitions apply as well to parents, subsidiaries, and affiliates. (For an exception to each of those generalizations see notes F and G to the appendix table.) The effect of one exception has been neatly illustrated by the commission:

> [A] person who initially gains control of a common carrier
> can subsequently acquire control of a freight forwarder, but a
> person cannot first acquire control of a freight forwarder and
> then acquire control of a common carrier; a person who
> acquires control of a common carrier and a freight for-
> warder, in that order, cannot later acquire control of another
> common carrier, although the common carrier controlled by
> such person can acquire control of another common carrier.[4]

The commission was addressing only the "absolute" prohibitions in notes F (and G) and L. If the mode of the second carrier differs from that of the first, one of the other notes would also apply as indicated.

One may well ask whether there is any unifying principle in these rules, any common touchstone, indeed any reason for being. It has often been observed that each rule originated in a need, as

---

[2] See appendix table, note D.

[3] See, for example, *Southern Ry, infra,* appendix table, note B; and Illinois C.R.R.–Control–John I. Hay Co., 317 I.C.C. 39 (1962).

[4] 76 I.C.C. Ann. Rep. 209 (1962). The commission recommended to Congress that the "uncertainty and confusion growing out of the provisions in question," §§ 411(a) and 411(g), be removed by putting freight forwarders under ICA § 5. That has not been done. See appendix table, notes F and L.

perceived by the Congress, to protect a particular mode.[5] True, but the protectionist encounters have been of three kinds—each based on different reasoning, all of it faulty.

In the first encounter, Congress sought to protect the conceived but unborn Panama Canal. The theory was that rich and powerful railroads would buy up shipping companies, divert their traffic to rail, and leave the Panama Canal bereft of tolls. The devised preventive was to preserve the independence of the Panama Canal users and their coastal and inland connectors, thereby preserving intermodal competition. Obviously anachronistic today, the reasoning was wrong in its time.

First and foremost it ignored the fact that the two modes each had advantages and disadvantages. The water carriers were there precisely because some shippers were willing to wait—even for passage around Cape Horn by sail—to obtain a lower rate. The opening of the canal would, of course, make intercoastal water carriage even less costly and less disadvantageous in speed. Nevertheless, the rationale was that railroads would try to attain total diversion, or at least enough to recover in monopoly profits what had been lost, by buying water carriers and liquidating them (without fostering new entry) and by predatory pricing to destroy what could not be bought and to bar new entry.

The second major flaw in the effort to protect the Panama Canal was that Congress ignored the vitality of the Sherman Act. Its constitutionality had already been upheld by the Supreme Court,[6] and the administration of President Taft had used it to break up the Standard Oil trust.[7] Similarly, the general authorities already given to the ICC

---

[5] For more extensive treatment of industry conditions at pertinent times, and related legislative goals and policies, see Robert C. Lieb, *Freight Transportation: A Study of Federal Intermodal Ownership Policy* (New York: Praeger, 1972). See also, Harold A. Horowitz, "A Review of Lieb's 'Freight Transportation,'" *Bell Journal of Economics* (1977), p. 715; Samuel P. Delisi, *Legal and Regulatory Aspects of Coordinated Transportation Service* (Pittsburgh: University of Pittsburgh Press, 1966).

[6] Northern Securities Co. v. United States, 193 U.S. 197 (1904) (not an invasion of rights reserved to the states).

[7] Standard Oil Co. v. United States, 221 U.S. 1 (1911) (after four and a half years of litigation). See also, United States v. American Tobacco Co., 221 U.S. 106 (1911) (requiring the breakup of J. B. Duke's ill-gotten empire).

The two cases solidified President Taft's position as a trustbuster. They also brought to a dramatic close one of the most curious and fascinating divisions within the Supreme Court, which had dated back to 1897. The battle was waged over two issues which, while logically unrelated, served as trade-offs.

An 1897–1898 majority of five had declared that when Congress proscribed "every contract . . . in restraint of trade" it meant "every." Adherents to that view tended to read "restraint of trade" as limited to those practices encompassed by statutes in the reigns of Edward VI and George III, which had largely found acceptance in the common law of the states.

were ignored. Had they and the antitrust laws been examined and found inadequate in this respect,[8] less draconian remedies could have been devised.

A second kind of encounter can be characterized as a sort of grandfatherly delight in a newborn infant—air commerce. Congress seems to have assumed the infant would mature best if it were given the right opportunities (air mail and passenger subsidies) and entrusted to the care of an agency not distracted by other cares. It charged the CAB with responsibility for developing air commerce and fostering a healthy industry.[9] Congress also gave the CAB authority, which it used, to exclude railroads from the air carrier sector and, for some seven years, from air forwarding. The theory of excluding railroads from air carrier ownership was that they would, somehow, use their financial strength to stunt the infant's growth. Why they would do so is as unclear as how, but every conceivable scenario invokes some of the comments already made about the exclusion of rails from water carriage.

There is one difference. In the first case Congress sought to prevent diversion from water to the stronger railroads. Here Congress was trying to hasten diversion, or at least protect against interference with diversion from the stronger carriers. It is clear that money can support a lot of bad habits, like rebating. It is also clear that money could not buy speed on the ground to match speed in the air. Lavish spending could have enhanced rail's initial advantages (comfort, reliability) and money could even have been used to malign air carriage. But the likelihood of any of that happening would, if anything, have been decreased by permitting rail investment in air carriers.

Pending legislation would cure what has become a deficiency in the congressional attitude toward air carriers. The CAB's charge to develop air commerce would be put into the context of our established

---

The dissenters, who eventually won, held that a restraint on *competition* was a restraint of trade, even if achieved by a device not outlawed by Edward or George; but the result, if not the logic, of that broadened reach was tempered by the view that only unreasonable restraints were illegal. Although Justice Holmes rarely thought it worthwhile to write a dissent, the first proposition brought him out fighting: "Great cases like hard cases make bad law" (Northern Securities Co. v. United States, *supra,* n. 6 at 400). "The [Sherman] act says nothing about competition" (*id.* at 403).

The significance of the shift from the English straitjacket ("restraint of trade") to the broader, more flexible concept seems to have eluded the Congress. Congress also slighted both the vigor of the Roosevelt-Taft attacks on the largest monopolies and the resolve of the Supreme Court in approving divestiture as the remedy. Indeed, Congress must have assumed that shipping monopolies would be formed and operated with impunity: it prohibited Sherman Act violators from using the Panama Canal, 37 Stat. 568 (1912).

[8] In fact, within months section 19a was added to the ICA by the Valuation Act, 37 Stat. 701 (1913); and the Clayton Act was enacted the next year, 38 Stat. 730 (1914).

[9] FAAct § 102, 49 U.S.C. § 1302.

national policy of developing all modes to make optimum use of the inherent advantages of each.[10] It would also open up entry without singling out surface carriers for different treatment.[11]

Encounters of the third kind were had with unruly adolescents: motor carriers, surface forwarders, and air forwarders. Separately, in weak and chaotic condition, they sought protection against their own excessive infighting. The prescribed cure was rest—preservation of the status quo. To make sure the convalescents were not disturbed, the alleged big bullies (railroads) were fenced out or fenced in. The regulatory agencies watched over the recoveries, limiting movement until health was restored.

Each of these cases might be likened to one of the two previously discussed. Diversion to rail was feared to some degree in each case. Financial strength was feared at least in the case of motor carriers and surface forwarders. But in each case it was feared that railroads would use their money and muscle to succor and support what they owned, to the detriment of their single mode competitors. This fear is markedly different from the concern in the case of rail-water carriers and rail-air carriers that railroads would use their wealth to buy and then destroy what they bought.

There is another way of stating the same dichotomy. In the two cases of rail-water and rail-air, Congress was concerned solely with intermodal competition. With motor carriers and air and surface forwarders, the concern was intramodal competition. Moreover, both concerns were exclusive: there was not any recognition of the possibility that a change in one form of competition—inter- or intramodal—may directly change the other. Had the railroads been permitted to cast their money upon the waters connected by the canal, they might have strengthened the industry and thus the intermodal competition.[12] Probably a creditable case could be made that intramodal motor competition by rail-owned carriers has over the years enhanced motor-rail competition.[13]

A final shared element of the motor carrier and forwarder cases is concern for protection of individual firms. It is impossible to still

---

[10] See S. 2493 § 2(a), S. Rep. No. 95-631, 95th Cong., 2d Sess. (1978), 51-52. This legislation was enacted as P.L. 95-504.

[11] See S. 2493 § 8, S. Rep. No. 95-631, 75-80. See also P.L. 95-163 (1977 all-cargo air service amendments to FAAct, appendix table, note E).

[12] Railroad money might, for example, have accelerated conversion from coal- to oil-fired steam.

[13] Accelerated investment again may be a possibility, both from rail profits and from enhanced accessibility to capital markets. See also the *Long-Haul* case *infra*, appendix table, note H (surface carrier entry into air forwarding added competitive stimulus). In any event, the case for intermodal facilitation is premised, as is the case for competition itself, on the proposition that as each player does more of what it does best, and less of what it does worse, everyone gains.

all argument about the merits or vices of that. It does seem appropriate to make one observation about the argument, with a return to a familiar refrain.

When it is argued that if a strong or rich outsider (a railroad or airline) owns, say, a motor carrier, the outsider will first destroy intramodal competition and then weaken or even destroy intermodal competition, one should always ask: By what means, fair or foul? If it is by fair means, is there any reason not to expect new entry, a replacement of the less efficient by the more efficient? Protection of motor carriers was sought and given precisely because entry had been free and easy. If foul play is the predicted path to superiority, again the focus should be on the antitrust laws and the general authorities of the regulatory agencies.

It seems cruel to close by listing the unifying principles of the existing rules of intermodal ownership: faulty analysis, anachronism, and overkill. A more hopeful note on which to end is that when multimodal *ownership* can, in fact, be expected to facilitate and increase intermodal *shipments,* the special rules can be read as substantially equivalent to the antitrust laws.

The principal congressional strictures, which have been added to the general rule against anticompetitive effects, are that the vehicles of the acquired or controlled mode be used by the acquiring or controlling carrier "to public advantage" and "in its operations." What should those phrases mean?

Recognizing that each mode has inherent advantages and disadvantages, Congress has in recent years stated, numerous times, a national goal of a balanced transportation system utilizing all the modes to best advantage.[14] Those statements should be taken as a flat rejection of the concept that intermodal ownership can be in the public interest only if the service of one mode is "auxiliary and supplementary" to that of another.[15] That is a master-servant relationship which

[14] Preamble to ICA, preceeding 49 U.S.C. §§ 1, 301, 901, 1001; Department of Transportation Act § 2, 49 U.S.C. § 1651 [hereinafter cited as DOT Act]. See also, U.S. Department of Transportation, *A Progress Report on National Transportation Policy* (1974), pp. 5-8 (collecting other statements of policy); *id*. at 10-11 (listing implementing legislation); note 15, below.

[15] In numerous cases, objectors have argued that the 1940 policy statement (note 14, above) required that single mode carriers be protected against the threat of competition from a multimodal carrier. That argument gained some measure of approval in the Supreme Court (see *American Trucking Associations, infra,* appendix table, note C). Indeed, the argument has prevailed even when the protection had the effect of preventing expansion of the more efficient mode, thereby preserving the inefficiencies of the objectors' mode. Central Truck Lines, Inc. v. Pan-Atlantic S.S. Corp., 82 M.C.C. 395, 406 (1960) (dissenting opinion).

Those precedents should not be regarded as controlling today, for the 1940 statement does not stand alone as the congressional statement of national policy on intermodal relationships. Later enactments show, unmistakably, a policy of building

might be conducive to balance but is certainly not necessary in all cases, if in any.

Further, the congressional declarations should be recognized as defining, in three significant respects, the older statutory terms. First, the congressional declarations assume a need for modal shifts in traffic, both to correct imbalances and as a dynamic process of adjustment to changes in traffic, technology, and other factors. Accordingly, a modal shift as a result of a proposed transaction cannot be regarded as per se contrary to the public interest. Second, while it seems reasonable to require an affirmative showing that a modal shift will be cost- or service-advantageous, it should not be necessary to demonstrate other "public advantage." Finally, since modal shifts are encouraged, the statutory requirement that a proponent carrier use vehicles of the new mode "in its operations" must be read as meaning its operations as adjusted in the congressionally favored directions.

It is of course true that a multimodal transaction may have anticompetitive effects, in some cases unrelated to the benefits of multimodal coordination and in other cases because of such benefits. The point is that fear of anticompetitive effects should not obscure, and even preclude, separate analysis of all significant effects—on transportation efficiency (in both service and costs), on access to capital markets and other benefits, and on competition.

Once the competition analysis is undertaken, it should be apparent that the issues are really the same as in antitrust cases in unregulated industries. For example, suppose two railroads and three barge lines

upon the efficiencies of each mode, with resulting marketplace elimination of inefficiencies. Cf. Department of Transportation, *Progress Report,* p. 8; P.L. 95-163 § 16(b), 49 U.S.C. § 1302(b); S. Rep. No. 95-631, 95th Cong., 2d Sess. (1978). These pronouncements are of three kinds.

First are the declarations of policy, starting with the DOT Act § 2, 49 U.S.C. § 1651. Another is found in the National Environmental Policy Act of 1969 (NEPA). It directs all federal agencies and officers to reexamine all existing rules and policies (§ 103, 42 U.S.C. § 4333) and to interpret all laws consistently with the NEPA goals, which include conservation and alternative uses of resources (fossil fuels) (§ 102, 42 U.S.C. § 4332).

Second, Congress has shown its favor by funding intermodal facilitation. This has included not only the efforts of DOT and other agencies but also intermodal facility projects. See, for example, DOT Act § 4(h), (i), 49 U.S.C. § 1653(h) (model intermodal terminal), (i) (preservation of railroad stations for use as intermodal terminals).

Finally, and most important, in authorizing single mode projects Congress almost invariably directs the planners to take into consideration the other modes. See, for example, 23 U.S.C. §§ 105(g), 134–35 (highway planning); Airport and Airway Development Act of 1970, § 3(a), 49 U.S.C. § 1702 (airports); Regional Rail Reorganization Act of 1973, P.L. 93–236, § 202(b)(2) (planning of Conrail to take account of alternative fuel efficiencies); National Mass Transportation Assistance Act of 1974, P.L. 93–503, § 102, amending 49 U.S.C. § 1602 (requiring state and regional multimodal planning).

compete to haul grain from A to B. An acquisition of the largest (by traffic in this market) barge line by the larger (same sense) railroad might significantly increase market concentration, while an acquisition by the smaller railroad might improve market structure. The analysis called for in either case is that of a classic horizontal merger. Suppose, instead, the barges haul from A to B where the rails compete for carriage from B to C. The issues are those of a vertical merger, if one of the railroads seeks to acquire a barge line. The other railroad would be effectively foreclosed from the market for the traffic of the acquired barge line. The analysis of the marketplace significance of that foreclosure might show that the smaller road would gain more traffic than it would lose.

There are two assumptions made in standard antitrust analysis that cannot be made here. One is that new entry into a concentrated industry is always to be preferred over an acquisition or other transaction that forecloses potential competition between the parties. The other is that the social and economic gains from limiting market concentration will always outweigh losses from foregone economies. The latter assumption fails for two reasons. Limiting market concentration is usually seen as necessary to limiting market power, in order to avoid its misuse. In a regulated market there are other weapons against misuse of market power. Second, on the other side of the equation, the foregone economies may be much greater in the regulated industry, for the reasons that led to regulation in the first place.

Indeed, it is in recognition of these differences that cost- or service-beneficial intramodal transactions have been approved by the agencies over objections to anticompetitive effects. Moreover, when the transportation benefits are substantial and comparable benefits cannot be obtained by less anticompetitive means, agency approval can be sustained in the courts.[16]

---

[16] See, for example, Northern Lines Merger Cases, 396 U.S. 491 (1970); Penn-Central Merger Cases, 389 U.S. 486, 498–99 (1968).

APPENDIX TABLE

Federal Rules on Intermodal Ownership of Common Carriers

Controlled or Acquired	Owner or Acquirer						
	Rail-road	Pipe-line	Water carrier	Motor carrier	Air carrier	Surface for-warder	Air for-warder
Railroad	—	*	B	*	K	L	K
Pipeline	A	—	B	A	K	L	K
Water carrier	B	B	—	*	K	L	K
Motor carrier	C	D	D	—	K	L	K
Air carrier	E	E	E	E	—	E	M
Surface forwarder	F	G	G	G	K	—	K
Air forwarder	H	J	J	H	M	H	—

* There is no statutory provision nor established agency test, but see text at notes 2-3.

NOTE: The letters in each cell refer to the paragraphs that follow.

A. Part I of the Interstate Commerce Act defined "common carrier" to include pipelines for liquids other than water, ICA § 1(1)(b), 1(3)(a); but Interstate Commerce Commission (ICC) jurisdiction over pipelines did not extend to entry, mergers, or other acquisitions (ICA § 5(13)). The Department of Energy Organization Act, P.L. 95-91, transferred to the secretary of energy all ICC functions relating to oil pipelines (§ 306), except rates and valuation, which went to the Federal Energy Regulatory Commission (§ 402(b)). Three of the four largest western railroads have extensive pipeline operations (Santa Fe, Southern Pacific, and Union Pacific) and the fourth (Burlington Northern) owns 50 percent of a pipeline. Penn Central owned (and, since the establishment of Conrail, continues to own) Buckeye Pipeline.

B. Ownership of vessels and common water carriers with which the railroad or pipeline does or may compete is prohibited in ICA § 5(14). The ICC interprets this as referring to parallel service, or service at two or more common points, and actual or probable competition; it has frequently found ownership lawful when an inherent advantage of the water service made actual competition unrealistic. See *Southern Ry § 5(15) App'n*, 342 I.C.C. 416 (1972) (collecting cases), *aff'd*, 386 F. Supp. 799 (D.D.C. 1974), 421 U.S. 1006 (1975); *Katy*

Industries Inc.–Control–Cenac Towing Co., Inc., 342 I.C.C. 616 (1973), *rev'd on other grounds sub nom* Valley Line Co. v. United States, 390 F. Supp. 435 (W.D. Pa. 1975). The ICC has authority to permit ownership of vessels and carriers that do not use the Panama Canal, whether they do or may compete with the railroad or pipeline, on an affirmative showing of "advantage to the convenience and commerce of the people" and no reduction of competition (§ 5(16)). With shipper and community backing, Southern Pacific and three smaller railroads were permitted, in 1915–1917 decisions, to retain a handful of competing water lines. See cases cited in *Southern Ry, supra,* at n. 8; *Penninsular & Occ. S.S. Co.,* 37 I.C.C. 432 (1915), 38 I.C.C. 662 (1916). (In *Southern Ry* the commission probably meant to cite its 1915–1916 approval of retained ownership instead of its unique approval, in 1934, of a rail-owned water carrier's instituting a new service.) There apparently was no opposition. All other rail applications to own a water carrier meeting the ICC's definition of competition have been denied. In the *Southern Ry* case (*supra,* 342 I.C.C. at 441-42 [collecting cases]) the ICC found there was not and would not be any competition between Southern and its water (contract) carrier, but if it were wrong on that point common ownership would meet the § 5(16) test of public advantage. (In affirming the commission, the District Court found it unnecessary to consider the second point.) The commission's finding seems to have turned on the fact that Southern's water carrier would not be competing for existing river traffic but would be used only for new coal traffic from two mines, and thus there would be no diversion.

C. ICA § 5(2)(b) authorizes the commission to approve a rail-motor transaction if it "will enable such [rail] carrier to use motor vehicles to public advantage in its operations." The commission has interpreted this as permitting approval only if the motor operations would be "auxiliary and supplementary" to the rail operations and has read the same requirement into ICA § 207 governing new certificates. See, for example, *American Trucking Associations v. United States,* 355 U.S. 141 (1957); *cf.* note E. Consequently, rail-owned motor operations have, in essence, been limited to certain coordinated services, often with motor carriage being a substituted service, as well as to authorities eligible as of June 1, 1935, under a grandfather clause. A few general authorities have also been approved on a finding of "unusual circumstances" (lack or inadequacy of existing service). *American Trucking Associations, supra;* see also, *American Trucking Associations v. United States,* 364 U.S. 1 (1960).

D. Prior to 1940 all Part I carriers (railroads and pipelines) that wished to obtain an ICC exemption were required to show affirmatively that ownership of a motor carrier would be consistent with the public interest (Motor Carrier Act of 1935, § 213). That requirement later was made applicable only to carriers by railroad (Transportation Act of 1940, §§ 7 and 21(e), 54 Stat. 906, 924 (1940), amending ICA §§ 5(2) and 213(a)(1)), but that seems not to have changed the result in subsequent water-motor carrier cases. See *In re Puget Sound Truck Lines,* 66 M.C.C. 357 (1956) (new certificate restricted to auxiliary and supplemental service). *But see also Atlantic Coast Line R.R.* v. *United States,* 265 F. Supp. 549, 1967 Fed. Carrier Cases 81,878 (D. Ill. 1966) (§ 5(2) rail restriction inapplicable; affirmative showing of advantage not required).

E. The Federal Aviation Act (FAAct) provides that a surface carrier acquisition of an air carrier can be approved only if it would "promote the public interest by enabling such [surface] carrier to use aircraft to the public advantage in its operation" (§ 408(b)). The Civil Aeronautics Board has held that the aircraft use must be auxiliary and supplementary to the surface operations. *American Export Lines, Control of American Export Airlines,* 4 C.A.B. 104 (1943); *cf.* note C. Further, while holding that compliance with that requirement is not mandatory for a grant of new operating authority to a surface carrier, the CAB refused to open an investigation of sea-air relationships in foreign and overseas travel. *American President Lines, Ltd.,* 7 C.A.B. 799 (1947). The CAB said it had a duty to exclude surface carriers except in a case of public necessity (*id.* at 804). Since the 1977 amendment to the FAAct opened entry to all-cargo air service to anyone "fit, willing, and able," the foregoing now applies only to combination passenger-freight air service. P.L. 95-163, §§ 16-17 (November 9, 1977), amending FAAct §§ 101-02 and adding new § 418, 49 U.S.C. §§ 1301-02, 1388.

F. A surface freight forwarder permit may not be granted to any Part I, II, or III carrier (ICA § 410(c)). That prohibition does not bar applications by a parent, subsidiary, or affiliate of a carrier (*ibid.*), nor does it bar acquisition of an established forwarder (§ 411(g)).

G. See note F. Applications by persons other than a subsidiary or affiliate of a Part I carrier (in particular, a railroad) may be denied solely on the basis of competition with preexisting service (P.L. 85-176, 71 Stat. 452 (1957), amending ICA § 410(d)).

H. The test noted in E above is not applicable, but the CAB denied railroad entry until satisfied that it would not threaten air carriage—economically or otherwise. Railroads were at first regarded as economic threats. *Air Freight Forwarder Case,* 9 C.A.B. 473 (1948). Entry was later liberalized for railroads as well as for other carriers. The changes were made, according to the CAB, in the interest of promoting intermodal carriage, but it seems really to have expected its approval would on balance favor air carriage. *Airfreight Forwarder Investigation,* 21 C.A.B. 536 (1955) (policy of free competitive entry;

approval of rail-affiliate entry "will stimulate the growth of airfreight" (*id.* at 546)), *rev'd and remanded on other grounds sub nom ABC Air Freight* v. *CAB,* 391 F.2d 295 (2d Cir. 1968). Entry by a long-haul carrier will be denied if it would restrain competition or jeopardize competing air carriers or forwarders. See *ABC Air Freight Forwarders* v. *CAB,* 419 F.2d 154 (2d Cir. 1969). After five years of monitoring the effects of its entry policy, the CAB found positive benefits from participation by long-haul surface carriers and put them in "substantial parity with independent forwarders." *Long-Haul Motor/Railroad Carrier Air Freight Forwarder Authority Case,* Docket 26907 *et al.,* Opinion and Order no. 77-6-126 (June 27, 1977).

J. Pipelines and water carriers have yet to face the CAB for entry into air forwarding. As long as there are marked differences in the commodities typically carried, it may be difficult to persuade the CAB of potential increases in intermodal carriage or other benefit to air commerce (see note H).

K. In a pending case the CAB is, in effect, asserting jurisdiction over the holding company parents formed by Braniff, Flying Tiger, and United. *Air Carrier Reorganization Investigation,* Opinion and Order nos. 75-10-65/66 (Sept. 12, 1975), *rev'd and remanded, United Air Lines, Inc.* v. *CAB* [Holding Company Reorganizations], 14 CCH Aviation Cases 18,255 (D.C. Cir. Nov. 28, 1977) (no rational basis for acting in only one of three forms of diversification). If the CAB's view of its authority is sustained, its jurisdiction would extend not only to acquisitions by air carriers and forwarders and their parents, subsidiaries, and affiliates but also to subsequent transactions, intragroup or otherwise, that would or could affect the air carrier. On the other hand, the CAB has held that the special requirement of § 408(b) (see note E) is not applicable to an air carrier's acquisition of a surface carrier. *TransAmerica Corp.,* Docket 21413, Opinion and Order no. 70-9-54 (1970). ICA § 5 does not treat air carriers differently than noncarriers.

L. Prohibited, ICA § 411(a); but see ICC statement quoted in text above at note 4.

M. The CAB brought forwarders within its regulatory ambit by deciding that, although they were not engaged directly in air carriage, they were, indirectly, air carriers. *Railway Express Agency, Inc.– CCN,* 2 C.A.B. 531 (1941). The only distinction between direct and indirect carriers drawn by the CAB in ownership cases is noted in notes E and H above. One may hope that the CAB would avoid applying the rule in one direction, but not the other, of combining direct and indirect carriers. Its original reasoning in making the distinction supports nonapplicability in both directions. See also 1977 amendment to FAAct (note E) and text above at notes 14-15.

Consolidation: Key to Multimodal Freight Transportation?

Paul O. Roberts

The types of multimodal transportation are limited in theory only by the number of modes and their possible combinations. In addition to truck-rail (piggyback) and truck-water (fishyback), which inevitably come to mind when the term "multimodal" is employed, truck-air, rail-water, and air-water movements, though less common, are occasionally observed. There are also the more exotic three-mode combinations, such as truck-rail-water or truck-water-air, and, for the sake of completeness, pipe-truck, water-pipe-truck, and the like.

Many freight movements which technically involve more than one mode are not commonly regarded as multimodal. Rail shipments from a team track, for example, necessarily involve a prior truck movement. Airfreight always involves pickup and delivery by truck as does Plan II piggyback, which is usually considered to be multimodal.[1] It is not clear whether we are referring here to multimodal ownership or to multimodal operations, or to both. It is apparent that the term "multimodal" alone is imprecise and may even be misleading in the title above.

The Nature of the Problem

In attacking this issue, I would like to incorporate both uses of the term multimodal: ownership and operations. The nation's statutes governing the economic regulation of transportation of goods either prohibit a carrier from operating in more than one mode or create hurdles which the regulatory agencies have invoked to inhibit multimodal operations. The question addressed by this conference is, Would the nation's transportation system be improved if the barriers to multimodal ownership were reduced or eliminated? I feel that I must first ask and answer the question, Are there significant economic benefits to be gained from multimodal *operations*? If there are, we can then ask whether multimodal *ownership* is the way to achieve these gains to society.

The U.S. restrictions on multimodal ownership date from the period of rail domination of transportation. As late as 1934 rail com-

---

[1] For definitions of piggyback plans, see the appendix to this volume.

panies were the largest private enterprises in the United States. The specter of railroad monopoly has been perpetuated in the various pieces of transportation legislation which came out of the first half of the twentieth century. The Panama Canal Act, passed in 1912, was designed to impede combinations between railroads and water carriers. The legislative history shows the fear which Congress had that the railroads would operate "ships in mock competition with itself." [2]

The Motor Carrier Act of 1935 limited the scope of rail ownership of trucking and was incorporated into Part II of the Interstate Commerce Act, although a number of rail–motor carrier combinations were allowed to exist by grandfather rights. In the Transportation Act of 1940 only railroads were restricted in their ability to control trucking operations. The concern was that the financial strength of the railroads might be able to control the activities of small and weaker companies in other modes.

The same separatist view has been followed between air carriers and surface carriers. The Civil Aeronautics Board (CAB) has not approved combinations of trucks and air carriers, but it has approved other modes' control of airfreight forwarding companies in order to bring in outside financial resources.[3] As a consequence, motor carriers have gained financial control of several airfreight forwarding companies with no apparent adverse effects.

In addition to the constraints on multimodal ownership, there are regulatory barriers to multimodal operation. The complexities of the route and rate structure pose difficulties. The necessity to deal with more than one regulatory agency—Federal Maritime Commission (FMC), Interstate Commerce Commission (ICC), and CAB—is onerous and difficult for the carrier accustomed to operating in only one mileu. The constraints imposed by working within the commercial area for trucking or the rail or air terminal areas tend to limit the sizes of the markets served.[4] The difficulty of getting carriers to file joint rates, particularly if one of them can offer through service as a single carrier, is a considerable deterrent to securing multimodal service. Even the lack of regulation causes problems, as when commodities are exempt from regulation when shipped by truck but not when shipped by rail. The problem is that rail cannot respond quickly enough to changes in the free market rates.

---

[2] U.S. Congress, *Report from Committee on Interstate and Foreign Commerce,* H.R. 423, 62nd Cong., 2nd Sess., 1912.
[3] Harold A. Horowitz, "A Review of Lieb's 'Freight Transportation: A Study of Federal Intermodal Ownership Policy,' " *Bell Journal of Economics* (1977), p. 715.
[4] The recent changes in the commercial zones for trucking and the complete deregulation of freight moved by air will facilitate, but not eliminate, these problems.

In spite of the restrictions,[5] some intermodal companies do exist and some freight is moving intermodally. What is the record? How are intermodal companies and intermodal freight doing? The results in both cases are modestly positive, but not overwhelming.

Intermodalism is an old concept that has begun to emerge on its own only since the 1950s. The ICC clarified the regulatory status of piggyback in 1954 by ruling, among other things, that motor common carriers, private carriers, and freight forwarders could arrange for line-haul service from a railroad without the railroad's having to acquire motor carrier operating authority for the rail portion of the intermodal movement. The growth in piggyback since that time has been remarkably steady at an average of 13 percent a year, until the recent economic setback of 1974–1975 (see Figure 1). This is good, but not dramatic. The container revolution on the North Atlantic was much more rapid. The complete changeover of the liner trade to a small percentage of uncontainerized freight took less than ten years. The economics must have been much more compelling than trailer on flatcar (TOFC). In fact, the use of maritime containers eliminated the break-bulk operations at either end. In comparison, rail carload is already containerized. Perhaps roll-on, roll-off shipping in the domestic maritime movements is a more apt comparison. The market penetration of this clearly multimodal concept in the scheduled trade with Puerto Rico, Alaska, and Hawaii is more like that of piggyback.

The question of the importance of intermodal ownership to the success of the intermodal concept is hard to answer definitively. In the United States, where there are only a few multimodal companies, the record seems to indicate that there is more cooperation between separate modal companies in joint ownership than for single mode companies. In a study of intermodalism in integrated transportation companies recently undertaken at M.I.T., one very clear conclusion reached from examining published statistics of the less than twenty railroads that had established trucking operations under the grandfather clause is that rail-affiliated motor carriers used between two and six times as much purchased rail, water, or air transportation as did Class I motor carriers as a whole (see Table 1).[6] Another finding was that rail affiliates that were local motor carriers tended to purchase relatively less rail transportation than did affiliated long-haul carriers. The local carrier affiliates

---

[5] For a much more complete treatment of the entire set of restrictions see Robert C. Lieb, *Freight Transportation: A Study of Federal Intermodal Ownership Policy* (New York: Praeger, 1972).

[6] A. F. Friedlaender, O. G. Dicker, I. Goodman, and I. Harrington, "Intermodalism and Integrated Transportation Companies in the United States and Canada," Preliminary Research Report supported by the National Science Foundation Office of R. and D. Assessment, Massachusetts Institute of Technology, September 1977. Class I refers to firms with revenues of more than $3 million annually.

presumably concentrated more on pickup and delivery services. For the rail-affiliated carriers as a whole there was a clearly demonstrated strategy for many of employing the trucking affiliate in such a way as to enhance multimodal transportation services.

FIGURE 1

CONVENTIONAL AND PIGGYBACK CARLOADINGS
IN THE UNITED STATES, 1955-1976

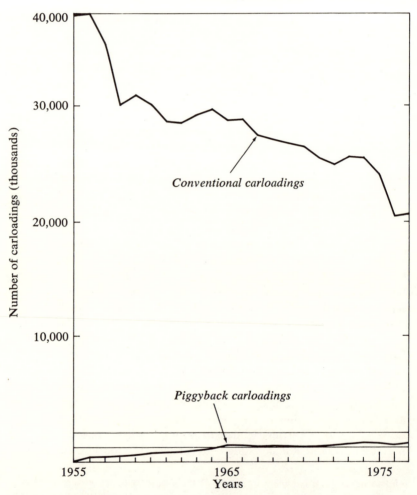

SOURCE: Transportation Association of America, *Transportation: Facts and Trends*, 13th ed., December 1976.

TABLE 1

TON-MILES, TONS, PURCHASED INTERMODAL TRANSPORTATION, AND
OPERATING RATIOS OF RAILROAD-OWNED TRUCKING FIRMS AND ALL
REPORTED COMMON CARRIERS, 1966 AND 1974

	1966	1974
Rail affiliates		
Ton-miles		
Total	1,069,983	1,217,347
Purchased rail, water, or air	121,030	190,325
Purchased as percentage of total	11.3	15.6
Tons (total, in thousands)	8,346	5,895
Truck-miles		
Total	140,366	117,586
Purchased rail, water, or air	10,437	15,294
Purchased as percentage of total	7.4	13.0
Operating ratio	96.7	100.5
All Class I carriers: General commodities		
Ton-miles		
Total	75,662,317	104,091,997
Purchased rail, water, or air	2,431,383	2,071,098
Purchased as percentage of total	3.2	2.1
Tons (total, in thousands)	242,965	272,298
Truck-miles		
Total	6,261,013	7,898,539
Purchased rail, water, or air	198,827	169,589
Purchased as percentage of total	3.2	2.1
Operating ratio	95.0	94.8

SOURCE: Friedlaender and others, "Intermodalism and Integrated Transportation Companies in the United States and Canada," Preliminary Research Report supported by the National Science Foundation Office of R. and D. Assessment, Massachusetts Institute of Technology, September 1977.

In Canada there is no barrier to simultaneous corporate ownership of the various modes. Both Canadian Pacific and Canadian National railways own large trucking affiliates which together perform between 15 and 20 percent of all Canadian trucking. The percentage of total rail traffic that goes by piggyback is larger in Canada than in the United States, and the Canadian railroads provide more Plan I piggyback than do U.S. railroads.[7] It is clear from talking with Canadian transportation executives that intermodalism also plays a larger role in transportation generally than it does in the United States. It would

[7] Ibid.

be an exaggeration, however, to claim that they feel that it is "the answer" in any total sense.

Why then do we not give intermodalism a go? There are, of course, regulatory arguments against it and opponents who argue that intermodalism would be a mistake. They believe that there are still rail carriers with considerable financial strength and the threat of monopolistic behavior. If these giants are allowed to enter into and compete with other modes on a multimodal basis, it is feared that predatory pricing would eliminate local competition and establish monopoly markets. Once these markets were secured, the competitive pricing of the multimodal era could be gradually phased out, and prices instituted by the railroads established in their stead. These are at least some of the arguments against allowing multimodal ownership. However, they ignore the continued existence of ICC regulation and the antitrust laws, which would be left to protect shippers and the public against anticompetitive mergers and combinations.

Others would say that it does not matter whether multimodal ownership is allowed since nothing much would change. They argue that there are not sufficient economic incentives in multimodalism beyond the established services to make the effort worthwhile. Therefore, we should proceed by asking and attempting to answer the questions: What would happen if the barriers to multimodal ownership were removed? Would institutional barriers still remain? What are the arguments for and against multimodalism?

The Basic Factors Involved

The first question is, What is there about multimodal movements or multimodal operations that makes them more economically attractive than single mode operations? Are there particularly appropriate ways of employing the separate modes to exploit the natural advantages of each?

Clearly, each mode has special features which make it attractive for certain operations. Air is fast but expensive. Truck is flexible, ideal for pickup and delivery of small loads, and usually quite rapid, especially for distances of less than 500 miles. Rail is less expensive for longer hauls and larger quantities, but it is typically slower and less reliable. Water is very cheap for large movements, but only where waterways are available. Pipelines are useful only for moving bulk goods between a limited set of origins and destinations and only for those commodities that can be fluidized or gasified for the movement. It would appear that the modes are already employed where they are individually best suited.

The key must lie in their use for the most appropriate portion of the movement of a single shipment. Shipments typically go through a pickup, a set of terminal operations, the line-haul movement, another terminal operation, and the final delivery. The employment of the appropriate mode for each of these operations must be the central focus of the point in question. Current rail carload operations perform all portions of the movement of a single shipment using rail equipment. Long-haul LTL (less than truckload) trucking operations use trucks (albeit of different sizes) for all portions of the movement of the LTL shipment. In fact, it is only the so-called multimodal modes—piggyback, marine container, and roll-on, roll-off—that use different modes for the same shipment.

The principal reason for combining modes lies in the economics of consolidation. For a given mode, the basic size of the vehicle sets limits on its capacity and establishes the fixed costs associated with the vehicle movement. If the entire fixed costs of a given movement must be borne by a single one-ton shipment, the costs per ton will include not only the fixed costs but the variable cost per vehicle-mile as well. As vehicle load increases, all costs are spread over more tons, and the total cost per ton falls dramatically. Lowest costs per unit are obviously achieved at the capacity of the vehicle. For most modes there are certain fixed costs associated with vehicle ownership and terminal operations. The more miles traveled on a given trip, the smaller these fixed costs of terminal operations will be per ton or per ton-mile. Low unit operating costs per ton-mile can be traded off against high fixed terminal costs if the trip is long enough. Both these costs are summarized in the curves of Figure 2.

The various modes demonstrate precisely these same types of economies with respect to shipment size and distance, but at different levels. A ship or a barge represents a large commitment in capital costs and manpower, but the huge capacity and low operating costs per mile bring the unit costs down to very low values per ton-mile. For rail the commitment to run a freight train between two points is large, involving not only ownership but also the switching and yard operations as well as the fixed crew costs. In most cases the low costs per ton-mile realized are less than those involved in trucking. The key, however, is the volume traveling. If the fixed commitment is large and the volumes small, the result will be ruinous.

The case for multimodal operations, therefore, involves consolidation of flows to realize the basic economies of the low-cost, high-volume mode used in the line-haul portion of the movement. In a nutshell, the choice is between using a single mode directly from origin to destination and using a multimodal combination—pickup by one mode for movement to a consolidation point where the single movement is combined with others for joint line-haul shipment to a deconsolidation point where the load is broken up and distributed to the final destination by the most

29

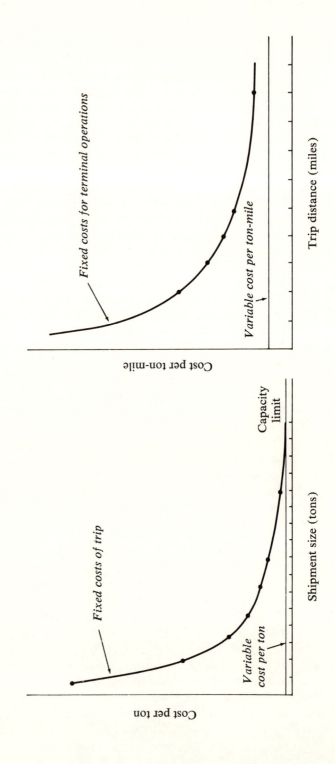

FIGURE 2

DECREASE IN COSTS PER TON AND PER TON-MILE WITH
INCREASE IN SHIPMENT SIZE AND TRIP DISTANCE

appropriate mode. The process (illustrated schematically in Figure 3) involves use of a consolidation terminal and its hinterland from which the freight is drawn. Presumably, if enough shipments are drawn from the hinterlands of the two consolidation terminals, the volume can be built up to the point where the higher fixed costs of the line-haul mode can be spread sufficiently to realize lower line-haul costs.[8]

Obviously, for any given origin-destination pair, if direct shipment costs less than consolidated shipment, the consolidated mode will not be used, unless the service is markedly better. The size of the two hinterlands is extremely important since it indirectly controls the volume of total tonnage that can eventually use the consolidated leg of the total movement. If the relation between tonnage and costs per ton-mile is as crucial as I believe it to be, the consolidated leg will have lower costs than the direct movement only when a threshold volume is achieved. That is, at volumes above a certain threshold, costs will exist at a competitive level. A greater distance between the two hinterlands also will assist in bringing consolidated line-haul costs down low enough relative to those of the direct mode to make consolidation practical.

If the size of the two hinterlands is too small, the volume of flow able to use the consolidation point could be less than the threshold volume. Methods of increasing the hinterland area may then be sought. It is also possible to design networks of consolidation points that generate high volume on the consolidated legs by aggregating volumes from various origins and destinations over the network. Figure 4 shows ways this can be accomplished. In Figure 4a, instead of shipping only between A and B, the leg between these points will also have shipments from A to C and A to D. The leg from B to C will have dropped shipments destined to B from A, but picked up shipments from B to C and D. In Figure 4b a multistage network consolidates shipments from A to D, E, and F into the break-bulk terminal at 1. At 1, flows to D and E are sorted out, flows from B and C are added to those from A, and the

---

[8] The costs for direct shipment are:
$$\text{TONS} \cdot [\text{CST}/\text{TONMI}_{\text{Mode 1}} = f(\text{TONS})] \cdot \text{DIST}_{\text{Direct}}$$
where: $\text{TONS} = $ quantity shipped
$$[\text{CST}/\text{TONMI}_{\text{Mode 1}} = f(\text{TONS})] = \text{cost per ton-mile by Mode 1 as a function of quantity shipped}$$
$\text{DIST}_{\text{Direct}} = $ direct distance between origin and destination.
The costs of consolidated shipment are:
$$\text{TONS} \cdot \{ ([\text{CST}/\text{TONMI}_{\text{Mode 1}} = f(\text{TONS})] \cdot \text{DIST}_1) + \text{HAND}/\text{TON}_1 +$$
$$([\text{CST}/\text{TONMI}_{\text{Mode 2}} = f(\text{TOTAL TONS})] \cdot \text{DIST}_{\text{Line-haul}}) +$$
$$([\text{CST}/\text{TONMI}_{\text{Mode 3}} = f(\text{TONS})] \cdot \text{DIST}_3) + \text{HAND}/\text{TON}_2 \}$$
where: $\text{HAND}/\text{TON}_{1,2} = $ handling costs per ton at consolidation points 1 and 2
$\text{TOTAL TONS} = $ the consolidated tonnage moving between consolidation points 1 and 2 $\text{Mode}_{1, 2 \text{ and } 3}$ are the various modes involved, and $\text{DIST}_{1, \text{ Line-haul, and } 2}$ are the various distances involved.

31

FIGURE 3

ELEMENTS OF THE TRADEOFF BETWEEN DIRECT AND CONSOLIDATED MOVEMENTS

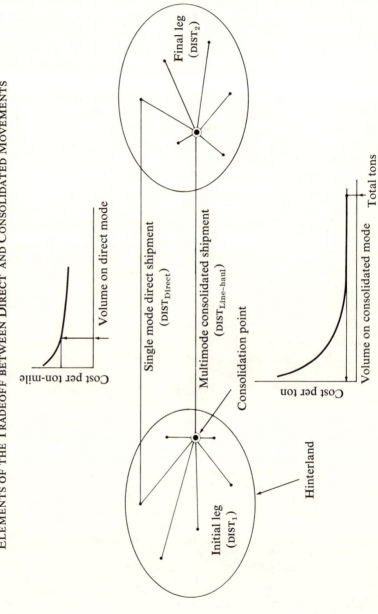

FIGURE 4

NETWORK METHODS OF AGGREGATING
LINE-HAUL VOLUMES

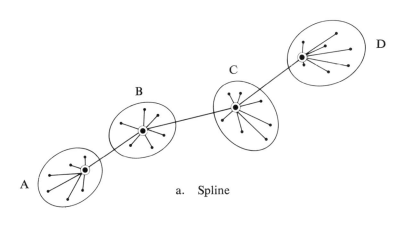

a. Spline

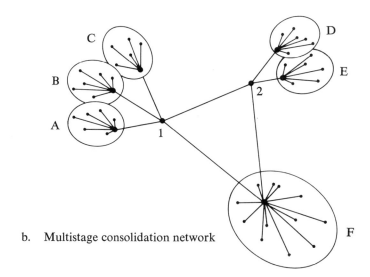

b. Multistage consolidation network

consolidation is sent on to F. A similar set of operations is performed for flows destined to 2.

Obviously, what I am proposing is no different from the consolidation currently undertaken by many of the successful individual carriers. Many railroad systems employ run-through trains that function like the spline system in Figure 4a.[9] Most long-distance trucking firms use

---

[9] See R. L. Banks and Associates, "Study of Merger Alternatives: Run-Through Trains," Report to the Rail Services Planning Office, Interstate Commerce Commission, September 21, 1977.

break-bulk networks like those in Figure 4b. Federal Express, an air parcel carrier that began operations only a few years ago, serves more than fifty of the major cities in the United States using a single consolidation-deconsolidation terminal in Memphis, Tennessee. Flights from each city by Dessault Falcon Jets rendezvous in Memphis where the contents are stripped, sorted, and repacked into the appropriate plane for the final destination.

The existing multimodal carriers also perform this type of consolidation function. Consolidation, particularly in truck-rail operations, may be more necessary than it is in single mode operations, however. Direct shipments by truck are already relatively efficient, and a carrier who controls all parts of the operation may be essential if the multimodal service is to compare favorably with that for direct shipments by truck. Multimodal movements will necessarily involve more handling than direct shipment. They are likely to be more circuitous because of their deviation from a direct path, and the inevitable delays in the consolidation operations require careful control if they are not to get out of hand. This control and coordination can best be handled by a single management organization because in every case the cost/service trade-off must be carefully balanced if customers are to be attracted on the one hand and profits are to be made on the other.

A Numerical Example for Truck-Rail

Because of the general interest in achieving better truck-rail coordination, considerable analytical work in this area has been done recently. Thus, the theoretical concepts discussed above can be illustrated by a specific numerical example.

The intermodal service offering I shall consider is referred to as a TOFC (trailer on flatcar) shuttle train. The specific prototype is the Sling Shot service inaugurated by Illinois Central Gulf on its 282 mile run between Chicago and St. Louis in 1976. The original concept was for a run-through piggyback train, using labor and equipment dedicated —that is, assigned exclusively—to this service between the two cities, and offering expedited, next-morning service in competition with truck. The train was to be operated by a reduced crew and carry at least ten flatcars (twenty trailers) in direct service, using a freight all-kinds rate of approximately $125 per trailer and, to the extent possible, using the shipper's own trailers. Because of the direct nature of the service, the operation would not require freight classification as would be the case if the flatcars were transferred from train to train at intermediate points. This would save both time and money.

This general type of TOFC service is not unique. A run-through piggyback unit train with somewhat these same characteristics has been offered by many railroads. For example, the Santa Fe's Super C service between Chicago and Los Angeles was quite well known. The Sling Shot's two-man crew appeared to be a unique and important feature of the shuttle train, so called apparently to exploit existing work rules. The general concept, however, is currently under active investigation by a number of research studies. Reebie's Integrated Intermodal Transportation Network and the Transportation System Center's Advanced Intermodal System both advocate essentially the same set of cost/service trade-offs.[10]

The problem with much of the current TOFC service from the user's point of view is that it is undifferentiated from ordinary rail service in its travel time. Too often it tends to get combined with ordinary rail carload service and is thereby forced through the standard classification process with all its delays and additional costs. When this happens it can no longer compete with truck effectively for time-sensitive commodities. The direct service proposed by the shuttle train concept is designed to be service competitive with truck at prices that are lower. The concept requires a sufficient volume of freight between the origin and destination in question to make a direct daily train possible. This may tend to limit the cities which can qualify for service.

To perform the analysis, the costs of shuttle train operations as a function of volume and distance are needed. A cost model of TOFC shuttle operations developed in conjunction with a research project performed at M.I.T. for the U.S. Department of Transportation was available.[11] The model develops both variable costs and fully allocated costs over different traffic volume densities and different distances for a range of load factors. The problem of joint costs is not as serious with TOFC shuttle train service as it might be when dealing with other rail services since the service employs mostly dedicated equipment and labor.

Assuming four-man crews, working under current 100-mile-day work rules, fully allocated costs, and a favorable load factor of 0.75, the costs for traveling between cities various distances apart were computed. To these line-haul and handling costs, a pickup and delivery cost of $75 per trailer was added to account for travel within the terminal area. The results are presented in the three-dimensional chart of Figure 5 in 1972 dollars per trailer-mile. It shows that unit costs per trailer-mile fall with both increasing traffic density and length of haul.

---

[10] Reebie Associates, *National Intermodal Network Feasibility Study,* prepared for the U.S. Federal Railroad Administration, Office of Policy and Development, Report no. FRA/OP PD–76/2, May 1976; and Transportation Systems Center, *Advanced Freight Systems Study, Phase I, FY '77,* prepared for the Advanced Systems Office, U.S. Department of Transportation (Cambridge, Mass., September 1977).
[11] Ralph D. Samuelson and Paul O. Roberts, *TOFC Shuttle Trains: A Study in Equilibrium Analysis,* M.I.T. Center for Transportation Studies, Report no. 77–9, June 1977.

FIGURE 5

COST VERSUS DENSITY VERSUS DISTANCE BY TOFC SHUTTLE

Cost per trailer-mile (in 1972 dollars)

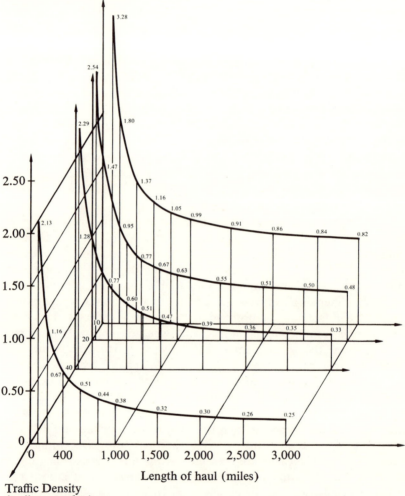

Length of haul (miles)

Traffic Density
(trailers per day)

For direct movement by truck the appropriate figures for comparison are those that would be avoided if the loaded trailer were shipped by TOFC shuttle rather than pulled by line-haul, over-the-road tractors. This includes the cost of the tractor, fuel, oil, tires, maintenance, and driver time, but not the cost of the trailer or the costs for pickup and delivery, terminal handling, billing, or administration. These operations must generally be performed whether TOFC line-haul carriage or truck is used. The problem of what cost to use is complicated by the fact that there is not one trucking industry with a single set of costs, but several with a range of costs.[12] There are regular-route carriers that specialize in less-than-truckload shipments, and irregular-route full-truckload carriers that use owner-operators on lease, for example, and private fleets of from one to several hundred trucks with a wide range of cost-influencing factors.

Obviously, no single set of costs is entirely adequate to represent the entire trucking industry, which ranges from the low-cost owner-operator to the inefficient private truck operator with his largely empty backhaul. With figures taken, in part, from a recent study on transport cost functions and from M.I.T. studies in progress on trucking costs, the range in costs can be defined and transformed into 1972 figures with deflation factors furnished by the American Trucking Associations.[13] Using typical load factors from an ICC study, effective costs per mile were developed for three sectors as follows:[14]

> Regular-route LTL general commodity carriers
> 1972 average cost per trailer-mile = $.516
> Typical load factor = 0.83
> Effective cost per trailer-mile = $.62
> Irregular-route truckload carriers
> 1972 average cost per trailer-mile = $.398
> Typical load factor = 0.83
> Effective cost per trailer-mile = $.48
> Private truck fleets
> 1972 average cost per trailer-mile = $.398
> Typical load factor = 0.60
> Effective cost per trailer-mile = $.66

The upper and lower limits of these cost levels are shown as planes in Figure 6. Together they span a significant portion of the range in trucking costs. For truckload operations the cost surfaces are relatively flat, as shown. Obviously, traffic density is much less important for truck than for TOFC. For LTL traffic, however, the markets are fragmented

---

[12] See Paul O. Roberts, "Some Aspects of Regulatory Reform of the U.S. Trucking Industry," paper presented to the Workshop on Regulatory Reform sponsored by the National Academy of Sciences, Washington, D.C., May 1976.
[13] C. E. Gill and H. O. Whitten, *Development of Transport Cost Functions,* Study prepared by H. O. Whitten and Associates for the Office of the Secretary of Transportation, August 26, 1976; and Paul O. Roberts, Thomas B. Brigham, and Carol A. Miller, *An Equilibrium Analysis of Selected Intercity Markets: Trucks with Double Trailers vs. TOFC Shuttle Trains,* M.I.T. Center for Transportation Studies, Report no. 77–25, December 1977.
[14] Interstate Commerce Commission, Bureau of Economics, Bureau of Operations, *Empty/Loaded Truck Miles on Interstate Highways during 1976,* April 1977.

FIGURE 6

Cost versus Traffic Density versus Distance by Truck

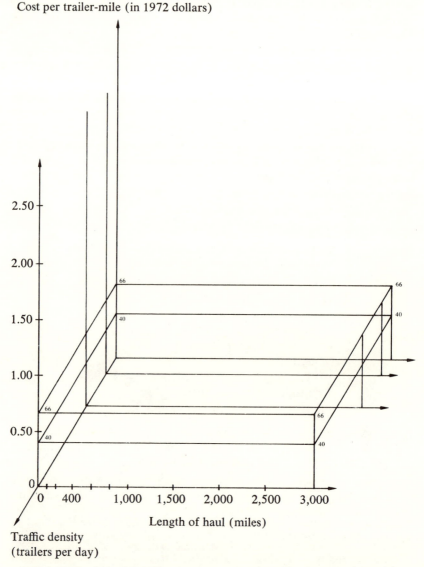

Cost per trailer-mile (in 1972 dollars)

Length of haul (miles)

Traffic density
(trailers per day)

over so many carriers that long-distance operators already have been
forced to a high degree of consolidation by the thinness of the markets.[15]

---

[15] The thinness of many markets is caused, in part, by the number of grants of authority that exist on some routes. For example, there are some seventy-two regular-
route carriers authorized to operate in the New York to Baltimore markets. These

Costs for this segment would be represented by a surface which slopes gently down in both directions from a high point in the left rear of the diagram where density and distance are least. This surface has not been shown because it is difficult to acquire data that allow precise definition of its shape and also because it is probably largely contained between the surfaces shown.

When the surfaces of Figure 5 and Figure 6 are placed on the same set of axes, their intersection produces a trace of the break-even traffic volume density required for TOFC shuttle train service at various lengths of haul. A summary diagram (Figure 7) of the break-even

FIGURE 7

BREAK-EVEN VOLUMES FOR TOFC SHUTTLE TRAINS
AT VARIOUS DISTANCES

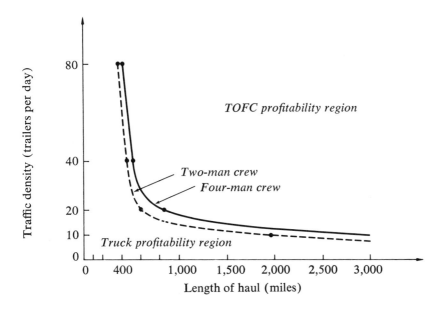

traffic density at various lengths of haul shows that extremely high break-even volumes are required at distances of less than 400 miles. For 500 miles volumes of more than forty trailers per day are required. Very low volumes (less than twelve trailers per day) cannot compete with present trucking technology at any length of haul. If the computations are repeated with two-man crews, the TOFC thresholds can be

carriers and any irregular-route, contract, and private carriers that are operating in this market are competing for approximately twenty-six truckloads of general freight per day.

Library of

Davidson College

dropped to ten trailers per day at approximately 2,000 miles. Once again, however, below approximately 380 miles the required traffic volume densities exceed eighty trailers per day. It remains to be seen whether two-man train crews can be realized throughout the rail industry generally. The importance of smaller crew size is clearly evident from examination of the curves in Figure 7. Reform of the work rules generally promises to be one of the major issues facing rail labor and management over the next few years.

Small changes in the important variables could shift these very speculative results rather dramatically. In fact, one of the most important of these variables, the TOFC pickup and delivery charges, is examined in more detail in the next section. Truck costs in particular cannot be treated as a single number. In the real world, the less-than-truckload sector has costs that tend toward the high end of the spectrum. The truckload movements, and particularly those by very efficient carriers, will tend to be at the low end of the cost spectrum. Nevertheless, the picture is clear. TOFC shuttle trains have an area of apparent dominance in long-haul and high-density markets. Trucking dominates the short-haul and low-density markets.

The Example in the Real World

To this point little has been said about service, but the whole concept of a TOFC shuttle is to give truck-equivalent delivery time and reliability. This can be done only by conscious and sustained effort on the part of rail management. If the TOFC shuttle cars must be put through the standard car classification processes, the probability that the service will deteriorate increases markedly. Costs, which for ordinary TOFC service have line-haul components down close to those for carload, would also begin to rise. Most important, however, truck-equivalent service would no longer be possible. Interconnecting traffic typically encounters too many service delays to be able to compete effectively. One is forced to conclude that in most cases a TOFC shuttle train must move from origin to destination in direct service to be competitive. That is, it should involve only a consolidating truck move to the terminal of origin, transfer to the rail flatcar, direct movement to the terminal of destination, and a deconsolidating truck move to the final destination.

For most moves the hinterland area is restricted to the "Railroad Terminal Area," defined in ICC regulations as the area around each city where rail-owned trucks may deliver freight as part of rail service. This zone varies in size from city to city, but it rarely includes more area than the SMSA (Standard Metropolitan Statistical Area) definition of the city and frequently not even that. This tends to limit the volumes available for movement. The extent of the limitation remains to be seen when the number and size of the intercity freight markets are considered.

Data on intercity freight movements in the United States are extremely sketchy. No single complete source of intercity tonnages is available. The Census of Transportation, Commodity Transportation Survey does cover the intercity movements of processed manufactures. Much of the individual commodity movements cannot be revealed because of restrictions on disclosure, but a tape for public use reports the estimated total tonnage by mode between twenty-seven production areas and fifty market areas. I have used it to prepare a matrix of origin to destination tonnages by mode for the most recent census, 1972 (Table 2).

The Census of Transportation figures have a number of limitations for the analysis presented here. Because the census does not distinguish TOFC services from other rail movements, it is impossible to identify, from this source, the volumes that are currently using TOFC. The survey covers only the products of manufacturers and ignores the considerable volume of agriculture and mining that moves by truck or, even more important, the volumes of manufactured goods that are handled through wholesale or retail distribution centers.

On the other hand, a considerable number of truck moves could not be handled by TOFC even if it were ubiquitously available. Some moves require very specialized equipment or handling. Some origins and destinations are too remote, and some operations too level-of-service sensitive to use TOFC. From the costs presented in the preceding discussion, it is clear that there will always be some irregular-route and private truckload carrier operations that are lower cost than TOFC. Truckload shipments by irregular-route carriers, for example, make up slightly more than half the total intercity truck ton-miles.[16] Thus, some fraction of the total of "common carrier truck" and "private truck" categories might be considered an estimate of the 1972 size of individual city-pair markets. For the sake of illustration, let us assume that the number added by increasing the scope of the census survey is equal to the number which would be removed from the potential markets by lower costs, specialized equipment, or level-of-service requirements. These truck flows which could be viewed as the source of market potential for TOFC are presented in Table 2.

Many of the markets shown in this matrix are zero or near zero. Others are quite large. Invariably, however, the large markets are over short distances. It is not immediately clear how many markets can meet

---

[16] Charles River Associates and Cambridge Systematics, Inc., *Potential Fuel Conservation Measures by Regulated Motor Carriers in the Intercity Freight Market,* prepared for the Federal Energy Administration, October 1976, App. A.

TABLE 2
ESTIMATED FLOWS OF MANUFACTURED GOODS BETWEEN SELECTED U.S. CITIES BY TRUCKS, 1972

(40-foot trailer equivalents per day)

Market Area	Production Area													
	1 Boston	2 Hartford	3 New York	4 Newark	5 Philadelphia	6 Baltimore	7 Allentown	8 Harrisburg	9 Syracuse	10 Buffalo	11 Cleveland	12 Pittsburgh	13 Detroit	14 Cincinnati
1. Boston	380	82	86	239	163	50	44	29	25	32	42	19	20	16
2. Hartford	101	112	111	172	90	29	41	9	27	22	25	21	10	10
3. New York	78	67	265	595	365	133	179	51	12	73	72	49	33	20
4. Newark	65	50	265	1045	631	169	234	41	64	0	108	80	44	25
5. Philadelphia	43	35	132	557	2552	222	217	134	15	52	91	91	49	17
6. Baltimore	9	17	40	149	204	157	37	55	3	11	41	74	14	12
7. Allentown	5	31	27	76	214	27	76	54	4	24	24	23	4	3
8. Harrisburg	12	8	17	74	213	108	82	189	4	8	36	34	8	7
9. Syracuse	18	16	55	100	69	19	29	14	82	49	45	17	33	5
10. Buffalo	16	22	34	74	106	10	21	20	35	970	117	56	87	32
11. Cleveland	19	20	18	56	53	22	12	21	31	62	930	266	262	108
12. Pittsburgh	10	8	19	45	100	32	11	14	3	21	239	280	79	25
13. Detroit	14	11	15	24	57	12	9	33	11	69	541	173	1253	156
14. Cincinnati	11	8	5	16	41	13	6	12	4	7	149	54	107	244
15. Chicago	26	28	34	68	51	26	11	19	30	40	224	170	279	125
16. Milwaukee	4	12	4	6	6	1	3	6	1	3	32	21	76	8
17. Minneapolis	4	2	5	6	9	2	2	4	3	3	29	9	18	14
18. St. Louis	6	3	8	17	10	2	1	3	3	3	26	20	46	31
19. Atlanta	9	12	15	24	22	4	9	9	5	7	25	10	21	21
20. Dallas	11	4	6	10	7	1	1	6	1	2	25	15	13	16
21. Houston	2	3	3	9	9	3	2	3	6	2	18	19	3	19
22. Denver	2	1	1	2	6	0	1	4	0	1	6	3	5	4

City														
23. Seattle	0	1	1	1	1	0	1	0	0	0	4	2	3	2
24. San Francisco	4	3	7	11	6	1	2	0	1	1	6	6	12	4
25. Los Angeles	7	10	21	17	18	3	4	3	5	2	20	3	25	14
26. Indianapolis	4	5	10	6	10	1	1	3	1	10	77	25	78	62
27. Kansas City	3	1	5	7	8	0	2	2	1	3	16	3	20	14
31. Scranton	3	1	4	10	10	186	9	2	5	8	1	2	1	0
32. Washington	6	8	17	85	99	26	8	4	1	10	29	6	21	4
33. Newport News	1	1	7	16	24	1	1	8	3	1	8	4	2	1
34. Columbus	4	3	3	16	11	1	2	5	1	4	94	48	53	50
35. Grand Rapids	3	1	3	3	6	1	1	3	0	6	26	8	82	20
37. Louisville	2	3	3	8	8	4	2	2	2	3	15	23	23	65
38. Nashville	5	4	2	8	3	0	0	1	0	4	9	4	6	20
39. Memphis	7	3	2	6	5	0	0	6	0	3	15	3	2	18
40. Augusta	1	1	2	4	3	0	1	2	0	1	2	2	2	2
41. Ft. Lauderdale	3	5	10	15	13	9	6	3	0	2	6	3	7	4
42. Birmingham	1	1	2	4	10	3	2	7	0	6	9	7	1	4
43. Tampa	3	2	3	7	4	0	3	2	0	9	4	1	2	7
44. Mobile	0	1	0	4	1	3	1	1	0	4	1	0	1	1
45. New Orleans	1	3	3	9	7	1	0	1	0	3	5	2	4	3
46. Omaha	0	1	1	1	4	3	2	1	0	2	9	1	3	2
48. Oklahoma City	1	3	1	2	6	0	1	0	0	1	6	3	5	8
49. San Antonio	2	1	1	2	1	0	1	1	1	0	1	1	1	2
50. Salt Lake	0	0	2	0	0	0	0	0	0	1	6	1	2	2
51. Phoenix	1	1	1	1	0	0	0	1	0	0	2	0	2	1
52. Portland	1	2	2	4	2	0	1	0	0	0	4	0	4	1
53. Sacramento	0	0	1	1	0	0	0	1	0	0	1	1	2	0
54. Fresno	0	1	0	0	0	0	0	0	0	0	0	2	0	0
55. San Diego	0	1	1	1	0	1	1	0	1	0	1	0	1	2
Total	911	614	1279	3618	5243	1288	1072	807	395	1535	3224	1666	2826	1232

43

TABLE 2 (continued)

Market Area	15 Chicago	16 Milwaukee	17 Minneapolis	18 St. Louis	19 Atlanta	20 Dallas	21 Houston	22 Denver	23 Seattle	24 San Francisco	25 Los Angeles	26 Indianapolis	27 Kansas City	Total
1. Boston	24	12	2	5	1	11	6	1	0	2	2	2	3	1299
2. Hartford	18	3	1	5	1	2	3	0	0	1	1	2	0	818
3. New York	45	10	20	8	1	4	12	4	1	3	5	6	2	2114
4. Newark	59	5	11	21	4	3	32	4	0	2	9	11	2	2983
5. Philadelphia	61	12	11	14	1	7	10	1	0	2	3	4	2	4335
6. Baltimore	25	3	10	3	1	2	2	0	0	0	3	1	1	873
7. Allentown	8	4	0	1	1	0	0	0	0	0	2	1	0	612
8. Harrisburg	11	2	0	2	2	1	1	0	0	0	1	2	1	822
9. Syracuse	17	5	1	1	0	2	0	1	0	0	1	1	1	583
10. Buffalo	43	2	3	6	1	7	3	1	0	1	3	7	1	1669
11. Cleveland	239	22	8	23	1	9	9	3	0	1	4	16	2	2216
12. Pittsburgh	75	4	4	3	1	1	4	0	0	0	2	3	0	984
13. Detroit	513	75	44	34	2	10	14	3	0	1	9	71	7	3162
14. Cincinnati	146	24	2	39	1	2	3	0	0	2	5	60	8	970
15. Chicago	2252	252	83	154	6	15	18	23	3	5	28	87	24	4078
16. Milwaukee	273	258	26	19	0	3	2	2	1	1	5	13	3	787
17. Minneapolis	112	20	66	17	1	4	5	2	0	3	4	9	17	367
18. St. Louis	201	10	9	276	0	6	7	6	0	1	3	25	52	774
19. Atlanta	27	9	3	11	57	7	7	2	1	1	7	14	5	342
20. Dallas	40	3	2	17	6	889	255	4	1	10	18	6	35	1403
21. Houston	27	1	5	11	1	221	763	1	0	7	13	3	12	1167
22. Denver	28	1	6	14	1	10	9	467	2	7	29	1	13	623
23. Seattle	5	1	2	1	0	5	1	2	224	31	28	0	1	317
24. San Francisco	23	3	2	4	1	3	4	15	13	1142	393	4	1	1670
25. Los Angeles	43	5	3	6	1	8	22	7	10	566	2491	4	3	3322
26. Indianapolis	166	16	2	49	1	1	3	2	0	0	4	70	3	610

														Total
27. Kansas City	54	3	3	117	0	24	8	10	1	1	8	12	236	563
31. Scranton	1	0	0	0	0	0	0	0	0	4	0	0	0	65
32. Washington	16	1	5	0	2	0	14	1	0	0	2	2	3	550
33. Newport News	13	1	3	15	5	6	0	0	0	0	1	1	0	124
34. Columbus	44	7	2	4	0	1	0	0	0	0	1	17	2	393
35. Grand Rapids	113	12	3	27	4	3	9	2	0	0	1	12	0	315
37. Louisville	65	4	5	4	13	3	1	0	0	0	2	31	3	315
38. Nashville	21	1	1	4	5	22	5	1	0	0	1	3	1	121
39. Memphis	29	3	0	17	5	1	2	0	0	0	5	6	7	168
40. Augusta	4	1	4	2	15	3	3	0	0	0	0	1	0	61
41. Ft. Lauderdale	10	3	1	8	20	3	9	0	0	0	3	3	1	136
42. Birmingham	15	1	0	3	26	3	9	0	0	0	1	3	0	108
43. Tampa	6	1	1	8	8	1	1	0	0	0	2	0	2	72
44. Mobile	2	0	4	1	12	1	18	0	0	0	0	2	0	52
45. New Orleans	12	3	1	3	3	15	28	6	0	0	2	1	3	120
46. Omaha	25	9	6	47	0	1	1	0	0	0	2	1	28	148
48. Oklahoma City	10	2	1	7	1	67	28	1	0	1	6	1	18	185
49. San Antonio	4	1	4	1	1	87	100	9	0	0	4	1	8	233
50. Salt Lake	4	0	0	0	0	1	0	3	2	15	35	0	1	79
51. Phoenix	9	0	2	0	0	10	2	1	2	28	206	0	2	274
52. Portland	7	1	2	1	0	3	1	2	34	44	33	0	0	152
53. Sacramento	2	0	0	1	0	0	1	1	3	306	75	0	1	397
54. Fresno	1	0	0	0	0	0	0	0	0	114	118	0	0	240
55. San Diego	2	0	0	0	0	0	1	0	1	35	363	0	0	411
Total	4951	814	376	1013	210	1477	1427	589	301	2336	3947	517	515	0

NOTE: In order to be consistent with the Census of Transportation I have retained its numbering of the market areas, although nos. 28, 29, 30, 36, and 47 are omitted from the sequence.
SOURCE: U.S. Department of Commerce, 1972 Census of Transportation.

the threshold limits on traffic density and length of haul set out in Figure 7. However, the production and market areas defined by the Census of Transportation tend to aggregate several SMSAS. Boston, for example, includes Worcester, Providence, Pawtucket-Warwick, Brockton, Lowell, and Lawrence-Haverhill. This aggregation inflates the size of the markets in relation to the current definitions of rail terminal areas.

Table 2 gives a reasonable indication of the density in the truck markets from which the TOFC shuttle service must currently draw. After the markets with a density of less than eighty trucks at less than 400 miles or fewer than twenty trucks at 600 miles have been eliminated, however, the number of markets is considerably reduced. Astonishingly few potential markets therefore appear in Figure 8. Some of the markets shown are on the borderline; others miss qualification because distance is insufficient or volumes are slightly too thin, but they might nevertheless be candidates after careful consideration. The commodities moving also bear consideration: some will not leave their current distribution system. For most of the city-pairs shown, if the market must be divided between several competing railroads, the game is lost—the volumes will be too thin. Many railroads are afraid that reducing their TOFC prices to truck-competitive levels might divert currently profitable carload traffic, and they have been reluctant to mount serious TOFC operations and marketing efforts. In view of all these constraints, it is fairly easy to understand why TOFC has not "taken off" to date. However, many of these constraints could be eliminated.

The most clear-cut finding, at least as I see it, is the constraining effect of the terminal areas. Many of the markets could be aggregated to reach threshold level if trucks could extend the pickup and delivery leg by 200 miles or so. This would greatly enlarge the hinterland area and allow threshold volumes to be reached in many more places throughout the country. At present, however, the only rail TOFC service that can use trucks in this pickup and delivery function beyond the terminal area is Plan II ½, in which the shipper arranges for travel to and from the railroad TOFC ramp. That this is the most popular piggyback plan in the United States today is clearly shown in Table 3: almost 57 percent of the tons shipped used this plan. In Canada, where multimodal ownership is permitted, Plans I and II are more popular and Plan II ½ is almost nonexistent.

To illustrate the point more graphically, suppose that pickup and delivery by truck were allowed between Detroit, Cleveland, Pittsburgh, and Cincinnati on the one hand and Dallas and Houston on the other. The aggregation by truck of the flows between the two groups of cities would build sufficient market volume that a TOFC shuttle train that would attract truck traffic could be run direct for the 900 miles between Cincinnati and Dallas. The aggregate volume potential can be obtained

FIGURE 8

MARKETS IN WHICH VOLUMES EXCEED THRESHOLD LEVELS FOR TOFC SHUTTLE TRAINS

(in number of 40-foot trailer equivalents taken from Table 2)

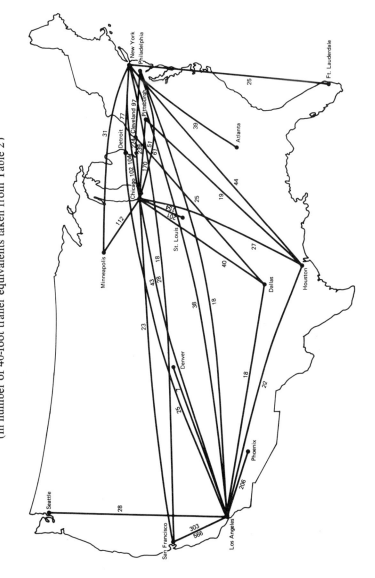

TABLE 3
FEATURES OF THE VARIOUS RAIL TOFC PLANS

Plan [a]	Equipment Furnished by	Service Offered	Tariff Publication by	Rates	Special Provisions	Notes	Usage [b] Millions of tons	Usage [b] Percent
I	Trucker	Point to point	Truck with division agreement	Commodity rates		IBT limitations [c]	3.9	8.4
II	Railroad	Point to point (within terminal zone)	Railroad	Commodity rates			6.2	13.3
II½	Railroad	Ramp to ramp PUD can be arranged [d]	Railroad	FAK [e]	Some commodities not FAK, mixture rules apply; non-mixed commodities at elevated rates	Empty sea containers sometimes moved free	26.5	56.7
III	Shipper	Ramp to ramp	Railroad	FAK		Sometimes empty gets ⅔ discount	3.3	7.1

Plan[a]					Rate basis	Percentage[b]	
IV	Shipper including flatcar	Ramp to ramp	Railroad Tariff Bureau	Two-trailer FAK	Two commodities, single-billed destination; volume discounts above twenty trailers	3.3	7.1
V	Carrier	Point to point; truck gets ramp to ramp	Joint truck/rail/truck	Optional commodity or FAK		1.1	2.3
Land bridge	Water carrier	Ramp to ramp	Joint water/rail	FAK	Single car, multiple car, and unit train / Flat fixed charge per unit train plus unit charge; empty gets 1/3 discount	2.4[f]	5.1
Total usage						46.7	100.0

[a] For description of plans, see appendix to this volume.
[b] 1974 figures from DOT, Federal Highway Administration, *Highway Statistics 1964–73/74*, table 9, n. 4; cited in DOT, *Summary of National Transportation Statistics*, June 1974.
[c] International Brotherhood of Teamsters Master Freight Agreement limits use by IBT unionized truckers.
[d] PUD=Pickup and delivery; available at prices ranging from approximately $50 to $100 per trip.
[e] FAK=Freight all kinds; rates excluded from some commodities.
[f] Other including land bridge.

by summing the appropriate elements taken from the census compilation of truck flows of Table 2. The summaries are shown in Table 4. Reference to the curves of break-even distances at various traffic volume densities presented earlier reveals that a TOFC shuttle could be operated at as little as 15 to 20 percent of the volumes shown. The problem with traffic volume density literally disappears.

TABLE 4

AGGREGATION OF TRUCK VOLUMES BETWEEN TWO
TRUCK-EXTENDED HINTERLAND AREAS

	St. Louis	Kansas City	Cleve-land	Pitts-burgh	Detroit	Cincin-nati	
St. Louis			26	20	46	31	$\left.\right\}\Sigma=176$
Kansas City			16	3	20	14	
Cleveland	23	2					
Pittsburgh	3	0					
Detroit	34	7					
Cincinnati	39	8					
	$\overbrace{\Sigma=116}$						

SOURCE: Table 2.

Markets could also be aggregated using the spline approach described earlier. For example, Houston-New Orleans-Mobile-Birmingham-Atlanta looks as though it might be a potential spline of interest. Current truck flows from New Orleans, Mobile, and Birmingham cannot be obtained from the Census of Transportation, however, because they are not listed as production areas but only as consumption areas. To make such a spline work care must be taken not to degrade service. A run-through train which stops only to drop off and pick up prearranged blocks of flatcars could work if properly scheduled. The term "through ports" has been coined to describe the concept of rapid through movements, without classification.

The most obvious way to eliminate the current constraint on truck pickup and delivery is to allow multimodal ownership of trucks by railroads. Not only would this have the effect of greatly enlarging the hinterland areas and, therefore, increasing the potential for traffic volume density, but also it should reduce, and perhaps even eliminate, the TOFC pickup and delivery charges. Pickups from the city of origin by truck could move directly to the TOFC consolidation terminal at the same line-haul cost, except for increased circuity, as direct origin-to-destination truck movements. In Figure 9 the break-even distances

FIGURE 9

TOFC SHUTTLE BREAK-EVEN VOLUMES AT VARIOUS DISTANCES,
CREW SIZES, AND PICKUP AND DELIVERY CHARGES (PUD)

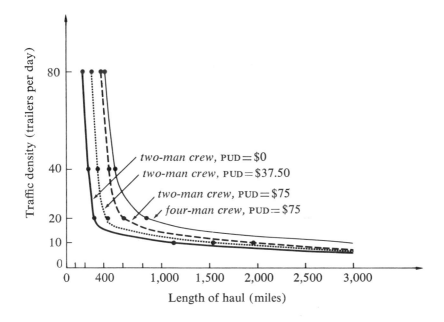

have been redrawn to reflect the impact of a substantial reduction in pickup and delivery costs. Within a single multimodal company steps could be taken by management to eliminate inefficiencies in the various segments of the trucking market.

If combinations of long-haul, regular-route LTL carriers and railroads were allowed, the urban area terminal collection and consolidation could be handled by truck in the city of origin as it is currently. The move from city of origin to break-bulk terminal would also be handled by truck. If break-bulk terminals were located adjacent to TOFC shuttle train marshaling yards, the line-haul function between break-bulk centers could be performed by TOFC shuttles. Many large LTL trucking firms have flows between break-bulk terminals which already exceed TOFC thresholds.

Other potential markets are the large private fleets and contract truckers. These movements could furnish the base to which less consistent movements are added to build toward a threshold level in any given market. Particularly in the short-distance markets, building up a threshold volume would be greatly facilitated by allowing railroads to enter into long-term contracts with shippers, including other carriers that might wish to use the service at reduced prices in return for guaranteed volumes rendered for shipment. Automobile parts and materials would be particularly suited to such an arrangement. Rail industry officials would argue that these commodities are already moving by rail at lower cost and should not be directed to TOFC. The crucial trade-off, of course, is between providing better service that attracts higher revenues and higher market shares overall or providing lower quality at a lower price in a smaller total market.

Freight forwarders could expand their use of trucks in broader pickup and delivery areas to take advantage of the TOFC concept described here. This would amount to doing for rail what the CAB did for air by allowing trucking companies to own airfreight forwarders. The question is whether trucking companies would want to own railfreight forwarders.

Other Advantages of Multimodal Ownership

The implications underlying the organization of this paper, so far, have been that if we can find economic benefits to multimodal operations which have not yet been realized, and if the barriers to achieving these benefits can be eliminated by allowing multimodal ownership, we have a prima facie case for allowing it. It seems to me that is precisely what has been shown. It could be argued that if there are ways to eliminate these barriers without multimodal ownership, they should be exploited either instead of, or in addition to, multimodal ownership. This leads to the question whether there are other benefits of multimodal ownership. For example, are there managerial or financial benefits beyond the operational benefits already identified? If there are, then there would be reason to allow multimodal ownership, even if there were no attendant operational benefits.

Managerial benefits of multimodal operations may include those attributable to marketing and market analysis. Knowing what various shippers have to move and being able to service the full range of movements would seem to be an advantage. Managing a full-service transportation company is extremely difficult, however, without separating it into operating divisions. For example, long-haul and short-haul trucking companies are reputed to be impossible to merge because of the differences in management strategies.

One managerial advantage might be the ability to phase out uneconomical services as technological change and shifts in the economy dictate the need. Thus, truck service could be substituted for rail on branch lines and the shift almost completely accomplished before the branch line is abandoned. This ability to shift would also facilitate the reemployment of personnel in new jobs and could promote less intransigence on the part of labor unions. Shifting both labor and capital to those places where they can be employed profitably would help to avoid problems of a sick industry.

Some advantages could accrue to a multimodal company if it were able to increase its geographical coverage or to develop more flexibility in its operations. For example, service between points A and B might for some period be performed from origin to destination entirely by one mode. Then, as volume levels grew to the threshold stage, the operation could shift over to multimodal service without the shipper necessarily even knowing of the changeover. Or the service from A to B might allow flexibility in the choice of single mode or multimodal operations.

The financial benefits that might be enjoyed by a multimodal company can range from the advantages of size—assuming that a multimodal company would be larger than a single mode company—to increased insurance against technological obsolescence. If it is true that a multimodal company has the flexibility to move its labor and capital from less profitable to more profitable undertakings without protracted regulatory proceedings, then it should be much easier for such a company to obtain the capital needed for expansion and renewal, either through debt or equity mechanisms. In fact, that may be the principal financial advantage associated with multimodal ownership.

A closely related financial advantage to multimodalism may also be the stability afforded by countercyclical movements of the different modes. Ocean tankers, for example, can be exceptionally lucrative at certain points in the long-run shipping cycle. Trucking is profitable during a completely different period, more related to the national economic cycle. However, most freight modes tend to move together with the economic cycle.

Overall then, there are certain advantages to being a multimodally owned company over and above any benefits attributable to multimodal operations. The principal one would appear to be the ability to move labor and capital in response to shifts in the economy as they occur.

The Institutional Problems

Certain institutional barriers to multimodal operations should be examined. The principal problem of a multimodal company with a base in trucking appears to be one of acquiring the property. Most national long-haul trucking companies have greater geographical coverage than railroads do, and this coverage appears to be important to their consolidation operations. It is difficult to conceive of a single railroad that is situated to serve a set of markets as extensive as that of a long-haul trucking company such as Roadway or Pacific Intermountain Express (PIE). Perhaps a regional trucking company, such as St. Johnsbury or Dohrn, would find a rail carrier with equivalent geographical coverage, but the threshold distances may begin to be too small.

A second problem is with labor. The National Master Freight Agreement signed by trucking management with the Teamsters restricts the use of TOFC. If management still must depend on union pickup and delivery drivers and dock workers, it would be hard to ask senior long-haul drivers to step down in favor of TOFC trains. Companies using nonunion owner-operators tend to have widely dispersed markets, and most irregular-route carriers are not large enough and do not have the management depth to handle both truck and rail.

It therefore seems logical to have a multimodal company with its base in the railroad industry. Railroad management could probably handle trucking as a subsidiary more easily than trucking management could manage railroads. There will, of course, be some disagreement about this. A holding company that has both modes as subsidiaries is another possibility, although coordinating the modal operations to produce a truly multimodal service would be a problem. The best arrangement would probably be a company that managed only multimodal operations, but it is difficult to see how such a company could acquire the railroad trackage rights necessary for multimodal service. And the same arguments of scale hold as in the trucking case. With a base in the railroad industry, however, it appears possible to acquire sufficient trucking rights, either through acquisition of existing trucking companies or their certificates, or through reapplication to the ICC for rights as a multimodal carrier using rail TOFC. Starting from the beginning would also have the advantage of bypassing the union problem with line-haul drivers.

It is conceivable to think of a base for a multimodal company in modes other than rail or truck. The most probable seems to be ocean shipping. U.S. liner companies have previously functioned in this role. In fact, many of the intermodal concepts currently used today were originally developed for marine application. Even as a collector-feeder service for international marine shipments, a multimodal company could be extremely interesting.[17] The question of financial strength is not as apparent for water or marine ownership as it is in the case of trucking.

Regardless of where the base is located, the complexity of U.S. railroad management, caused in part by the Balkanization of the industry, suggests that a corporate form that allows the three modes to

---

[17] Air is also a possibility. Flying Tiger Line appears ready to offer such an international airfreight service now that domestic airfreight is unregulated and they can enter into any markets they want.

function with individual managements would probably prove to be the most effective. The principal objective is to allow multimodal operation so that integrated moves can be made. The problem with separate subsidiaries is getting them to work together efficiently.

If, as I have suggested, the true objective is multimodal operations rather than multimodal ownership, then it is conceivable that allowing U.S. railroads to enter into long-term contracts with shippers and other transportation companies at reduced rates, in return for guaranteed volumes of traffic rendered, could have the most beneficial effects of all.[18] This arrangement would facilitate the development of integrated transportation in situations where multimodal moves would bring economic advantages. Combinations of regional motor carriers using long-term contracts with railroads could then enter into long-haul transportation.

There are short-run costs for any institutional change that is proposed—for example, cargo-stuffing rules were an issue when marine containers were introduced—but such institutional problems tend to diminish over the long term. In the same way, the use of union drivers would probably eventually change if multimodal operations became feasible, but in the short term the problem would have to be dealt with. It may be necessary to pay higher wage rates or to include termination clauses in existing union agreements in order to gain the necessary long-term flexibility in work rules to allow the change to occur. If multimodal ownership or operation is judged to be in the public interest, the passage of the requisite legislation would be greatly facilitated if the changes affecting labor could be phased in. Concern for the best interest of all the parties that are involved is, of course, essential to success.

Concluding Remarks

Within the framework of this paper, it is impossible to assess all the potential benefits and costs to shippers of multimodal ownership and operations. For the example cited, a TOFC shuttle train, it appears that in certain markets this concept could be cost effective but that the existing structure of the U.S. railroad industry offers the biggest barrier to its successful implementation. A problem for many railroads is the lack of national or even regional coverage. Considerable reorganizing of the market areas served may be required before the concept can be made fully operational. If, as seems possible at this juncture, a new wave of railroad mergers were to produce truly nationwide companies, the possibilities for multimodal operation would be greatly

---

[18] See, for example, ICC ex parte 270.

enhanced. If, however, an increasing number of carriers were reduced to bankruptcy and integrated into regional, quasi-government organizations, the opportunity for multimodal cooperation probably would be reduced rather than enhanced. A strong, privately owned railroad system seems to be the most important precondition for a satisfactory multimodal arrangement.

It seems highly likely that, despite prodding by the administration, Congress will not move toward the complete deregulation of trucking. But considerable reform, short of complete deregulation, appears to be desirable to allow ownership or operation of multimodal companies, or both. If the economics of multimodal operations are attractive enough to bring about their initiation, then it seems likely that the industry will still have to be structured in such a way that present institutions can buy off the losers in the system. This should happen naturally if the legislation establishing multimodal companies or operations is properly structured.

As this paper suggests, a careful look at the economics will require detailed investigation of the demand side in conjunction with the supply side. The cost/service trade-offs inherent in all transportation operations are especially important to the multimodal concept, and unless both demand and supply are considered simultaneously, improper judgments as to economic viability are likely to result. The thinness of the various markets in the United States seems to require the use of consolidation terminals. Consolidation would make possible a greatly expanded role for those modes that achieve their best economies at higher densities. They seem to promise a more efficient, high-level transportation service overall. To be successful, however, these consolidation-deconsolidation operations will require both good design and creative management.

Multimodal Ownership in Transportation: A Canadian Perspective

Harvey M. Romoff

Multimodal ownership in transportation is a topic that has generated considerable controversy over the years, particularly in the United States. In direct contrast to the U.S. experience, there has been an almost unrestricted development of multimodal ownership in Canada. A fair question, and the purpose of this background paper, is to ask exactly what can be learned from the Canadian experience and how this might apply to the debate underway in the United States.

Philosophically, there are two broad ways to approach a question of public policy such as whether multimodal ownership should be permitted. The first, which I would call the "weak" argument, works from the premise that unless demonstrably deleterious effects on the public interest can be identified, a set of actions should not be disallowed. This approach lies close to the basic philosophical bedrock of Western society, but unfortunately it leaves many unconvinced in this age of growing governmental intervention in the economy. In particular, when a proposed public policy such as permitting multimodal ownership goes against a long history of statutory prohibitions, to say nothing of well-entrenched myths, the "weak" approach, even if made convincingly, is unlikely to carry adequate weight.

As a result, one is pushed to the second philosophical position which I would term the "strong" argument. This works from the premise that a set of actions should be permitted only if it can be demonstrated that positive effects on the public interest will result from their implementation. This, of course, places the burden of positive proof on those advocating change and makes the justification all the more difficult.

In this paper, I propose to review the development of multimodal ownership in Canadian transportation and, from this background, to address myself to both the weak and strong arguments for multimodal ownership.

The Canadian Regulatory Framework

Canada has a much smaller economy than the United States, which perhaps explains why Canada never thought it could afford to follow the

U.S. lead in competition legislation and regulatory practice. The structure of multimodal ownership in the Canadian transport industry developed unfettered by public policy constraints or specific statutory prohibition until the passage of the National Transportation Act in 1967. This legislation was the first attempt in Canadian history to deal specifically with multimodal ownership. Rather than to summarize the provisions, it is easier to quote the relevant text, which is clear and to the point.

> Section 27.(1) A railway company, commodity pipeline company, company engaged in water transportation, or person operating a motor vehicle undertaking or an air carrier, to which the legislative jurisdiction of the Parliament of Canada extends, that proposes to acquire, directly or indirectly, an interest, by purchase, lease, merger, consolidation or otherwise, in the business or undertaking of any person whose principal business is transportation, whether or not such business or undertaking is subject to the jurisdiction of Parliament, shall give notice of the proposed acquisition to the [Canadian Transport] Commission.
>
> (2) The Commission shall give or cause to be given such public or other notice of any proposed acquisition referred to in subsection (1) as to it appears to be reasonable in the circumstances, including notice to the Director of Investigation and Research under the Combines Investigation Act.
>
> (3) Any person affected by a proposed acquisition referred to in subsection (1) or any association or other body representing carriers or transportation undertakings affected by such acquisition may, within such time as may be prescribed by the Commission, object to the Commission against such acquisition on the grounds that it will unduly restrict competition or otherwise be prejudicial to the public interest.
>
> (4) Where objection is made pursuant to subsection (3), the Commission (a) shall make such investigation, including the holding of public hearings, as in its opinion is necessary or desirable in the public interest; (b) may disallow any such acquisition if in the opinion of the Commission such acquisition will unduly restrict competition or otherwise be prejudicial to the public interest; and any such acquisition, to which objection is made within the time limited therefor by the Commission that is disallowed by the Commission, is void.

The more interesting features of this provision are: (1) It applies only to acquirers who are subject to federal jurisdiction—that is, those who operate interprovincially or internationally. (2) The only grounds for disallowance of a proposed acquisition are that "it will unduly restrict competition or otherwise be prejudicial to the public interest." (3) The statute imposes very significant delays in the acquisition process which may be exploited by competitive acquirers who are not subject to the statute.

In the decade since the enactment of the National Transportation Act, there have been only a limited number of proposed acquisitions that fell within the scope of the statute, and few, if any, of these have been disallowed. Several acquisitions of small trucking companies by the major railways have been allowed, as has the acquisition by a major railway of a 50 percent interest in a company with the power to own and operate commodity pipelines and the acquisition by another major railway of a significant interest in a North Atlantic container-ship operation. Perhaps the single most significant result of the statute was totally unintended—the purchase by the province of Alberta of Pacific Western Airlines, a regional air carrier, following notification and public announcement that a company that was subject to section 27(1) intended to acquire the airline. Of course, it is not known whether any acquisitions have not taken place because potential acquirers have feared that their position could be preempted by third parties during the time lag between notification and actual acquisition or that proposed acquisitions would be disallowed. But a reasonable conclusion is that the 1967 legislation has not yet significantly altered the structure of the Canadian transport industry.

In general, the regulatory framework in transportation within Canada has historically been much less burdensome than in the United States. There is no federal regulation of the intercity trucking industry, only provincial regulation, and it is generally much less onerous than U.S. federal regulation. The attitude toward railway pricing is much more permissive in Canada than in the United States, particularly since the passage of the 1967 transportation legislation. There is no economic regulation of international shipping.

Canadian Pacific

Canadian Pacific, the most fully multimodal enterprise in the world, began as a railway, but from the outset it had a strong intermodal bias. The main line of the railway across Canada was completed in 1886, the first transcontinental line in Canada. Now called CP Rail, it has over $1 billion in total annual revenues.

In the same year the transcontinental railway was completed, Canadian Pacific began chartering ships on the Pacific Ocean to connect with the railway. This start was followed by the acquisition of an interest in shipping in the Atlantic to connect with the eastern terminal of the railway. Before the end of the nineteenth century, Canadian

Pacific offered an integrated through-service between Western Europe and the Orient. Over the years, the company's ocean-shipping interests developed in their own right in response to changes in trade patterns and technology, as well as to the loss of most of the fleet in two world wars. Today, Canadian Pacific has two wholly owned subsidiaries— CP Ships, which operates a fully containerized service between Quebec City and the United Kingdom and the Continent, and CP Bermuda, which was formed in 1964 to engage in all aspects of international deep-sea shipping. CP Bermuda today has a fleet of some thirty vessels with an overall deadweight of approximately 2 million tons, which are operated under various types of charter and affreightment arrangements.

The Canadian Pacific's involvement in the trucking industry began in 1884, while the railway was being built, when the company purchased an express company which later became CP Express. From its beginning as a wagon stage, this operation developed into an integrated, local trucking and intercity rail, small shipment service. The development in Canada of intercity trucking lagged behind development in the United States because of lower population density, longer lengths of haul, and the later development of adequate highways. Immediately after World War II, however, it became clear that this mode would become a major part of the domestic transportation scene. Beginning in 1946 Canadian Pacific engaged in a series of acquisitions that, coupled with growth from within, has made it, through various subsidiary companies, the largest intercity trucker in Canada, with a market share of something under 10 percent. It ranks as one of the larger common carrier truckers in North America.

In 1919 Canadian Pacific obtained statutory authority to own and operate aircraft within and without Canada. Beginning in 1939, it acquired a series of small regional airlines, mostly bush lines operating north and south, and in 1942 it formed Canadian Pacific Airlines Ltd., now called CP Air. From these beginnings, CP Air has evolved into a major domestic and international air carrier.

The only major sector of the transportation industry in which Canadian Pacific has, at present, no operating involvement is the pipeline sector. Its interest is limited to a research program in the pipelining of solids and ownership of a significant share of TransCanada Pipelines, the major west-east trunk gas pipeline in Canada. To round out the picture, CanPac International Freight Services Ltd. was incorporated in 1972 as a wholly owned subsidiary to provide various transportation-related services. This includes customs brokerage, sufferance and dry cargo warehouses, freight forwarding, and various agency services. Transportation represents only one facet, albeit a major one, of Canadian Pacific's interests, however. The company also has substantial operating and investment interests in telecommunications, hotels, in all aspects of the resource industry, and certain areas of manufacturing. Over the past twenty years, these nontransportation interests have formed the larger part of Canadian Pacific's development thrust.

In capsule form, the consolidated sales of the company are in the order of $4 billion, of which some 45 percent is in the transportation sector and 55 percent in other industries. In the transportation sector, the railway accounts for some 55 percent of sales. In 1976 the transportation interest of Canadian Pacific earned approximately 6 percent on capital employed while the nontransportation sector earned about 12 percent.

The Structure of the Canadian Transportation Industry

The major multimodal enterprises in the Canadian transportation industry are Canadian Pacific, which is shareholder-owned, and Canadian National, a crown corporation fully owned by the federal government. Both enterprises grew from railways, which should not be surprising since railways were the first major domestic transport mode and were for many years the country's largest business. The railway share of the overall transport market has steadily decreased, however, because of changing technology and market forces.

Canadian National has lagged far behind Canadian Pacific with regard to multimodal development. Over the past two decades Canadian National has developed a major trucking subsidiary, largely by acquisition, and more recently has purchased a major interest in a North Atlantic container-shipping operation. Air Canada, the country's major domestic and international flag carrier, was formed in 1936 as a subsidiary of Canadian National, but for some time it has been operated as an independent government-owned airline. Legislative changes late last year formally separated the government ownership in Air Canada from Canadian National.

Other examples of multimodal owership in Canada are few and limited. A major Great Lakes carrier owns one of the country's major trucking companies; certain smaller railways have developed their own trucking subsidiaries and, in certain instances, domestic shipping operations. But Canada is a small country with only two Class I (major) railways and two Class I (trunk) airlines. The scope of multimodalism is obviously limited by the nature of the country and its transportation industry.

What is the state of competition in Canada's transportation industry? The two major railways are transcontinental and serve all major industrial areas. There are regions which are captive to a single railway, but these are limited. Within the trucking industry, there is fierce competition nationwide with the players ranging from large national trucking companies to small regional companies and local firms. There are two major airlines and several regional carriers, but in aviation competition has been carefully limited by federal government policy, although a steady liberalization is taking place.

Unfortunately, there is no simple thermometer to measure the health of the competitive process in Canadian transportation. In view of the choice given to the user, both inter- and intramodally, the pricing flexibility enjoyed by the carriers, and the very nominal returns being earned by the carriers, a reasonable conclusion would be that the competitive process is working well and that the competitive structure of the industry is not inappropriate to the geography, demography, and economic structure of Canada. I do not think that there are many in Canada who would quarrel with this assessment.

The Weak Argument

The weak argument in favor of multimodal ownership is that it should not be disallowed unless it can be clearly demonstrated that deleterious effects on the public interest would result from its allowance. There can be no doubt that evidence from the Canadian experience shows that no deleterious effects on the public interest have resulted from multimodal ownership in transportation.

Multimodal ownership in Canadian transportation has not been destructive to competition or to anything else. If the public interest has been in any way harmed, there has been a remarkable scarcity of complaints. In a country only about one-tenth the size of the United States, as measured by population or economic activity, two very large transportation enterprises operate without any serious suggestion that competition within the transport sector suffers or that the public interest suffers in any other way. It is difficult to see why the results should be any different in the very much larger and more vigorous U.S. economy.

True, there was a period when common carrier trucking groups took strong exception to railway expansion into the intercity trucking industry, but I believe it is fair to say the Canadian trucking industry no longer fears it will be gobbled up by the railroads, or that railroads will use their trucking firms to destroy the trucking industry. Not only would this represent a form of economic insanity, but it could not succeed, given the obvious ease of entry into the trucking industry. Certainly the users of transportation are not dissatisfied with the structure of the industry, and I cannot recall any suggestion by a shipper that the structure of the Canadian transport industry was in any way unsatisfactory. The concept of multimodal ownership is not an issue among Canadian transport users.

The Strong Argument

It is unfortunately not so simple and straightforward to use the Canadian experience in making a positive case for multimodal ownership in transportation. The problems are both conceptual—how to define the public interest—and analytical—how to measure the impact of multimodal ownership on the public interest.

Carrier Profitability. One simple, but obviously incomplete, measure of the public interest might be the economic health of the transport industry as measured by its profitability. Does the Canadian experience suggest that multimodal ownership results in a healthier, more profitable transport industry? No clear conclusions can be drawn, at least on the basis of known data and analytical techniques. The significant test should be Canadian Pacific—the most multimodally integrated enterprise in the world and one that is shareholder-owned. Return on invested capital in Canadian Pacific's transport investments is only some 6 percent, about half the return on its nontransport investments. The difference, of course, partly reflects certain situations unique to Canada, such as the statutory rates on export grain movements which remain at their 1897 level and produce a shortfall of several percentage points in return on overall rail investment.

But, despite extenuating circumstances, nothing in the Canadian experience suggests that multimodal ownership has been a panacea or magic answer to the problems and difficulties facing the transport industry. Indeed, there is little factual basis on which to conclude that multimodal ownership has made any significant difference at all. The fact that the major development thrust of Canadian Pacific over the past several decades has not been in transportation strengthens this conclusion. One would like to think that the impact of multimodal ownership on carrier profitability has been positive, and several reasons for thinking so will be dealt with later, but the factual position remains unfortunately blurred.

Intermodal Handling. Another simple and incomplete measure of the public interest could be the development of multimodal traffic handling in a country's transport system. (For clarity, I will refer to traffic handled multimodally as intermodal traffic.) Given the extensive documentation in support of the proposition that the present modal split poorly reflects the comparative costs of the various modes, it would appear that increased intermodal handling would reduce the overall economic cost of providing required transport services. One can thus argue that the public interest is benefited as intermodal transport increases its share of the overall transport market.

To measure the benefits of multimodal ownership it is necessary to examine the linkage between multimodal ownership and intermodal transport. Two separate issues are to be considered: the *economic logic* of why and how vertical integration in transport might lead to increased intermodal traffic, and the *factual question* of whether, in fact, this occurs.

Economic logic offers support for the proposition that multimodal ownership in transportation will increase intermodal handling of traffic. So long as the regulatory process significantly interferes with market pricing and prevents modal prices from reflecting economic costs, it follows that a multimodal transport owner will do better than the marketplace in making intermodalism happen, since he can internalize costs which are not reflected in market prices. Put another way, the vertically integrated transport operator should respond to economic costs while his nonvertically integrated competitors will respond to market prices which are distorted by the regulatory process. This argument can be presented rather elegantly in mathematical form, but its intuitive logic is quite straightforward.

One obvious way in which to deal with the factual question of whether vertical integration in transport leads to increased intermodal handling is to compare the inroads of intermodalism in Canada and the U.S. The data present difficut problems in such a comparative analysis, but the limited work that has been done seems to indicate fairly convincingly that intermodal handling developed earlier and more rapidly in Canada than in the United States and now constitutes a larger share of the transport market in Canada than in the United States.

There is thus a strong temptation to accept the reasoning that multimodal ownership leads to increased intermodal handling, which leads to a more efficient modal split, which in turn benefits the public interest. This reasoning is based on some fairly simple economic logic coupled with a factual comparison of the inroads of intermodal handling in Canada and the United States. But there are serious pitfalls in this series of propositions. To appreciate fully the Canadian experience and its lessons, one should understand these pitfalls. The first has to do with the assumptions implicit in the economic proposition that vertical integration in transport leads to increased intermodal handling. The second has to do with the conclusions which should properly be drawn from a comparative study of intermodal development in Canada and the United States. Each will be dealt with in turn.

Vertical Integration and Intermodal Handling

The economic logic linking vertical integration and increased intermodalism is unassailable, but it depends on two key assumptions, both of which have become less and less valid for the Canadian transport scene today. The situation was substantially different in the 1960s and totally different in the 1950s. It follows that economic logic is better used in explaining why intermodalism developed first and more quickly in Canada, rather than why intermodalism is more prevalent in Canada today.

The first assumption is that the regulatory process significantly distorts the relationship between prices and costs in the transport sector. With the virtual deregulation of rail pricing in 1967 and the failure to develop a federal regulatory policy for intercity trucking, however, it is increasingly difficult to argue that significant distortions between prices and costs still exist in the Canadian transport industry, at least insofar as multimodal traffic is concerned.

Five major characteristics of Canadian intermodal pricing that have evolved in recent years distinguish it from U.S. practice: (1) separation of rates for intermodal maritime traffic from those for domestic traffic; (2) widespread attention paid to round-trip rates and imbalanced traffic flows; (3) numerous rates published to apply only to named customers; (4) a variety of volume-related rates, usable by numerous or only by individual customers; and (5) the vigorous competition offered by Plan II piggyback, given the wide rights the railways hold to pick up and deliver traffic.[1]

The second assumption is that the vertically integrated transport owner can internalize those costs which are not reflected in market prices and so perform "better" than his nonvertically integrated competitor. That is to say, the multimodal transport owner will be able to operate as an integrated whole, centrally allocating traffic between modes and either ignoring modal profit and loss statements or operating a system of shadow prices. At Canadian Pacific, with which I am familiar, this integrated approach was employed at the outset, but it has given way to a highly divisionalized approach consisting of almost totally independent profit centers. The pattern of development of Canadian National, the other major multimodal operator, has been similar, although lagged.

When Canadian Pacific first took a significant position in intercity trucking, it operated its subsidiary trucking companies as adjuncts to the railway. There were instructions to use railway Plan I piggyback services for specified hauls, to limit trucking marketing effort in those areas where the railway was the dominant carrier and the traffic was attractive to the railway, and to price with due regard to published rail tariffs. It did not take long to find out that this was simply not workable. It distorted incentives, yielded meaningless managerial control documents,

---

[1] For definitions of piggyback plans, see the appendix to this volume.

and destroyed any type of managerial accountability and responsibility. It was found that the trucking companies were not being efficiently operated, that their service level was inferior to that of their competitors, and that limiting the marketing thrust of the railway-owned trucking companies to protect the railway did not really help the railway at all because there was no lack of other truckers waiting to attack. And attack they did, with some considerable success.

Today, CP Transport is very much a self-standing trucking company, able to choose where and when it uses Plan I piggyback services, where it should concentrate its marketing efforts, and how it should price its services. Quite naturally, it is expected to use CP Rail Plan I piggyback services as opposed to those of the competitor, other things being equal, and to use the services of CP Air and CP Ships, other things again being equal, as opposed to those of competitors. But it pays tariffs for these services—either the standard published tariffs or others negotiated very much at arm's length. Anyone could make the same deal with other transport arms of Canadian Pacific as CP Transport does, given the same volume and other conditions surrounding the movement of the traffic.

In general, Canadian Pacific is convinced that the concept of self-standing profit centers for each transport mode is the only workable organizational structure for a large intermodal transport enterprise. There are several reasons for this. (1) Intermodal traffic still makes up a fairly small portion of the overall business of any single modal entity, with the exception of CP Ships. Therefore, it makes no sense to let the tail wag the dog by organizing around intermodalism. (2) There is an overwhelming need to give local authority and responsibility to each of the modal profit centers and let their managements operate their own business as they see fit. Each mode is different from the others and requires dedicated and specialized management, able to respond to situations quickly and effectively. (3) No one is smart enough to sit at the center of the web and direct operations in the various modes so as to achieve a rational, nonoverlapping transport system. This may be possible in certain industries (although this is far from clear), but the dynamics, constant change, and need for immediate decisions in transportation make this totally impractical. (4) Modal marketing, with all its overlap and conflicts, permits a higher degree of market penetration than does centralized multimodal marketing. The extra costs resulting from the overlap are easily covered by greater market shares.

The result, not surprisingly, is a fairly loosely structured transportation company. Each self-standing independent profit center is judged on its performance and its own profit and loss statement. Each one operates independently and markets and prices independently. Each uses the services of other arms of the company where it chooses to, at prices in published tariffs or negotiated directly; each is allowed to use services provided by third-party transportation companies where it is clearly to their advantage; and there is no need to justify such decisions daily to corporate management. This is not an empty freedom.

The decision to divisionalize was not made lightly. One factor taken into account was certainly the great increase in pricing freedom after 1967. It is a moot but interesting question whether a multimodal transport operator would have followed the same path if faced with pricing restrictions of the type found in the United States.

Divisionalization does not imply chaos. A strong corporate management sets overall policies and guidelines, allocates capital and people, and sorts out those conflicts that need sorting out. Considerable stress is placed on fostering the flow of people between corporate management and the profit centers and among the profit centers themselves. Indeed, the flow of people among the various entities and the esprit de corps that derives from membership in a large family may well be one of the strongest factors favoring intermodalism.

Canadian–U.S. Comparison

The second pitfall along the path between multimodal ownership and intermodal traffic has to do with the somewhat simplistic conclusion that the observed greater market penetration of intermodal transportation in Canada can be directly attributed to the greater vertical integration in the Canadian transport system. While there may be some validity in this hypothesis, a host of different conditions exists in both countries, all of which can, and likely do, significantly impact the modal split of traffic. It would be naive in the extreme to postulate a simple causal link between vertical integration and intermodal handling. Some major differences between Canada and the United States are: (1) Rail and trucking firms are subject to detailed and pervasive rate regulation in the United States. These restraints do not exist in Canada. (2) Teamster restrictions on the use of Plan I piggyback are much more onerous in the United States than in Canada. (3) The highway network in the United States is more developed than in Canada. (4) Canadian manufacturing and industrial activities are much more geographically concentrated than in the United States. (5) The use of owner-operators does not appear to be as great in Canada as in the United States.

All these factors suggest that, regardless of the degree of vertical integration in transport, one would expect comparatively more intermodal transport in Canada than in the United States. A simple statistical comparison between Canada and the United States, therefore, should be treated with great caution.

Intermodalism in Canada: A Recapitulation

The tone of the last few pages has been perhaps too negative. A fair summary would be that the degree of price regulation in Canadian transportation, the managerial structure of multimodal firms in Canada, and inherent differences between the economies and institutions of both countries all prevent one from concluding, at least with a strong degree of confidence, that the greater use of intermodalism in Canada can be directly traced to vertical integration in the Canadian transport sector. An obvious corollary is that on the basis of the Canadian experience it cannot be argued with a strong degree of confidence that the United States would witness a surge in intermodal traffic if multimodal ownership were permitted.

On the positive side of the ledger, there is little doubt that multimodal ownership had a great deal to do with the earlier and more rapid development of intermodalism in Canada. This was due to the more imperfect pricing system which then existed and the more integrated managerial approach first taken. And at least of equal importance was the ability of the multimodal firm to break down the traditional hostility and distrust among the various modes. The modal cooperation necessary for intermodalism to develop was obviously easier to achieve within one firm than between competing firms.

The early and rapid development of intermodalism by the multimodal firms established a thrust and set a pattern which became self-sustaining, even when the regulatory pattern improved and the multimodal firms became divisionalized. The aggressive approach taken by the vertically integrated firms set an example which, of necessity, was followed by the rest of the industry. At present, there are managerial pressures favoring intermodalism in the vertically integrated firms, which cannot be dealt with by economic theory. Management has a multimodal flavor, often has had experience in more than one mode, and, by being part of a multimodal whole, has a natural inclination toward intermodalism. Management is also more professional. Though difficult to prove, it is likely that these managerial factors help the profitability of the integrated firms. Therefore, it should not be concluded that vertical integration in Canadian transport has not affected the development of intermodal traffic. The impact has been, and remains, considerable. Unfortunately, it does not work wholly through the mechanism postulated by economic theory, and it is not the type of impact that can be easily quantified and analyzed.

Two basic differences between Canada and the United States with regard to transportation policy are the vertical integration in the Canadian transport sector and the much less rigid regulatory approach to pricing in Canada. Intermodal traffic developed and exists in the shadow of both these factors. If forced to choose between the two—a most unreal situation—my interpretation of the Canadian experience would be that pricing flexibility was, and is still, the more significant driving force behind intermodalism. If by legislative fiat Canadian Pacific and the other Canadian multimodal firms had to spin off their transport holdings to separate and new owners, it is unlikely that there would be discernible changes in the way traffic is handled in Canada. Of course, there would be significant shifts between carriers, and the markings on the boxes customarily seen at certain places would change, but the overall national transportation scene would look little different. But if by legislative fiat the U.S. type of price regulation had been introduced in Canada one or two decades ago, it is very unlikely that intermodalism would have developed as it has, even with the vertically integrated firms. If, by some misfortune, such pricing controls were introduced now, a significant deterioration of the intermodal system could be expected, no matter what was done by the multimodal firms.

Summary

Multimodal ownership is not undesirable and does not in any way disadvantage the transport industry, transport users, or the public at large. If this is true in small Canada, it should be even more true in the large United States. It is difficult, however, to present conclusive arguments, based on the Canadian experience, that multimodal ownership positively affects the public good. Points in favor of this propostion should be as applicable to the United States as to Canada, but they tend to be qualitative rather than quantitative.

There are no panaceas or magic potions for the transportation industry. If a single answer is sought, the Canadian experience suggests that pricing flexibility has had greater significance for the development of intermodalism than has multimodal ownership.

PART TWO

PROCEEDINGS

Conference Discussion: First Session

First Topic: **How would carriers react to the elimination of statutory and regulatory barriers to multimodal ownership? Would they form multimodal companies?**

JOHN W. BARNUM, resident fellow, American Enterprise Institute: In welcoming you to this conference, I would like to express to each participant my appreciation and the appreciation of the American Enterprise Institute for taking your valuable time to focus on the issue of multimodal transportation companies. I have asked two or three people to introduce each topic, and although some have prepared papers on their topic, I will ask that they summarize rather than read them. I have also distributed each of the papers to two or three other people and asked them to be prepared to pick up the discussion on that topic. The floor will then be open for discussion by all of the other participants. I cannot think of a better person to lead off this conference than Ben Biaggini, so I shall ask him to start.

B. F. BIAGGINI, chairman and chief executive, Southern Pacific Transportation Company: The question I am assigned to address is: If the statutory and regulatory barriers to multimodal ownership were removed, would carriers proceed to form multimodal companies? In my opinion, this is exactly what would happen. I think we would see substantial expansion in the ownership of surface multimodal transportation companies. Undoubtedly, there would be some expansion in the field of air transport, involving airfreight forwarding, the extension of pickup and delivery limits beyond airports, and so forth, but the greatest opportunities exist in rail-truck and rail-barge lines.

Today the railroads and the highway carriers are pretty much tied to well-defined territories: the railroads, by the existence of their track and their historical geographical location, and the highway carriers by the route restrictions or the permission to use certain routes given to them by their ICC certificates. Looking at the whole spectrum of transportation, we can see that most categories of freight that move long distances can be handled by all-rail, all-truck, or by a combination of rail-truck, rail-barge, truck-barge, and so forth. Through the years, we have seen the evolution of a large number of coast-to-coast motor carriers. In fact, with my orientation principally toward railroads, I have the feeling that national policy has been to create coast-to-coast highway carriers and to inhibit the development of coast-to-coast rail carriers.

Some larger highway carriers do own barge lines and pipelines and, certainly, many highway carriers are entirely capable of owning and operating railroads. Railroad expansion through merger, however, has been quite limited by, first, the delays in handling merger cases and, second, the criteria that are applied to railroad merger cases under the existing statutes and regulatory laws. Railroads therefore have not experienced the same end-to-end consolidations that truckers have. After 150 years of railroading, there is still no transcontinental, single-line, coast-to-coast rail carrier.

If the multimodal restrictions were eliminated, I would expect rail carriers to compete for traffic beyond the geographical limits of their own operations and to try to get into the trucking business, either by organizing and developing their own trucking companies or, more likely, by acquiring existing carriers. Railroads, at first, would seek to extend their services into a relatively small area beyond the metropolitan pickup and delivery zones, out into the countryside. This, of course, would be a break from the old territorial concept. An end-to-end connection between railroad and truck line would eliminate the archaic notion of a particular territory being the province of a particular railroad company. I think there would be some pretty aggressive maneuvering by the railroads; through ownership of motor carriers they would try to extend their services into areas that they cannot reach with the physical plants they now have. In addition, I see railroads seeking to acquire parallel motor carriers that serve the same territory. I use the phrase "railroads seeking to acquire" because of my railroad background, but I see no reason some of the larger trucking companies would not be interested in acquiring railroads. Railroads the size of Western Pacific, for instance, might very well be picked up by highway carriers if that appeared to be advantageous.

In any case, the acquisition of a parallel motor carrier, or the consolidation of parallel highway and rail carriers, offers substantial opportunity to eliminate services that may be wasteful for the railroad under present circumstances and to develop alternatives with a combination of rail and highway. Substitution of truck services, for example, appears to be the most viable solution to the problem of weak branch lines that have become uneconomical for the railroads to operate. On Southern Pacific we have been able to eliminate over 2,500 miles of uneconomical branch lines since the end of World War II.

Our trucking subsidiaries, which provide substitute service, have been a valuable aid in meeting local apprehensions and some of the objections from regulatory bodies when we seek to close branch line facilities that have outlived their usefulness. These are examples of intermodal common ownership, acquisition, mergers, or other arrangements that we would see immediately.

I would also expect combinations to develop on the inland waterways. Certainly, for Southern Pacific, a merger with a good barge line would be a very attractive proposal. Most rail-waterway affiliations probably would be end-to-end rather than parallel because little would be gained by the substitution of either rail service for barge service or barge service for rail service between points that are common to both the barge and the rail.

The economics of the movement would govern which mode of transportation would be used. With end-to-end combinations, however, the economic advantages of the two modes of transportation could be combined to provide better and more economical service for the public. In addition, the management of the different modes of transportation—and this would apply also to the inclusion of a motor carrier in that group—under common corporate policies, with an overall philosophy of providing a department store of transportation, would be beneficial to the shipping and receiving public. In each case, I think that competition would be enhanced.

There is no doubt that an "invasion of territory" (to use the historical term) of a weak rail carrier by a strong rail carrier plus a strong truck line would have some effect on that weak carrier. By the same token, the weaker carrier can also develop its trucking activities and reach into new territory that its rails do not serve or that is served by the stronger rail carrier.

After an initial shakedown, the transportation companies and the shipping public would be accustomed to common ownership and common control of transportation. There would be a greater tendency on the part of shippers to deal with a truly versatile transportation company, one that could provide all its services under a common philosophy of rate making, furnishing of equipment, and so forth, and I feel that would be beneficial.

As for the organization of a multimodal group of companies, I would prefer to keep the corporate entities separate. That is, I would keep the trucking company, the barge company, and the railroad as profit centers under individual management. Each company would be free to cooperate where it was advantageous to cooperate and to compete where it was advantageous to compete. It would be important to continue to have the trucking managers think like truckers and the barge people think like barge people and the railroad people think like railroad people, with one overriding exception: They would know that their performance would be observed by a common owner and would be judged not only on modal profitability but also on the effectiveness of the modal group in working with the other modes to provide efficient services which maximize overall profitability.

At Southern Pacific we know that our customers look on transportation as a reducible cost, and we have tried to be responsive to that concern and to be as innovative as possible in the different modes we operate. Our primary interest and the largest part of our business is in railroads, but we also operate a large family of trucking companies. For many years our trucking operations were limited by the prior-and-subsequent-rail-haul and the key-point restrictions that were put on railroad-owned trucking companies in the early days. After years of litigation before the Interstate Commerce Commission, we have been able to get key-point and prior-and-subsequent-rail-haul restrictions removed from all the principal routes of the motor carriers, and now they are operating more like trucking companies than like a railroad affiliate.

We are also in the pipeline business and, of course, that is different from railroading. Nevertheless, our overall experience in transportation, the knowledge at corporate headquarters about what shippers need, how cases are handled before the regulatory commissions, and so forth, has been beneficial to the growth of our pipeline business.

Some critics say that common ownership stifles innovation. I would point out that we have the only operating coal slurry pipeline in the United States, the Black Mesa line. I think that our experience in multimodal transportation ownership has been beneficial not only to our company and shareholders but also to the public that we serve. With the elimination of the restrictions on our Pacific Motor Trucking Company, we have an opportunity to do even better in the trucking business.

If I were to list the problems of the railroad industry, I would not put barriers to intermodal ownership as number one. At this moment, I think that we should direct attention to providing more equality in transportation. Railroads should be given the opportunity to compete with other modes of transportation on an equal basis by such measures as extending to railroads the barges' bulk exemption and the truckers' exempt commodity list. In addition, I think there should be adequate user charges on facilities that are provided by the public sector. Southern Pacific's experience in the trucking business does not leave us at all afraid of having to pay a fair share of the cost of constructing and maintaining the highways. And if the ICC had let us acquire the John I. Hay Barge Company as we tried to do back in the late 1950s, we would not be worried about fair user charges on the waterways either.

I am all for common ownership and certainly would be supportive of any change in the laws that would make it easier for multimodal transportation companies to develop.

ROBERT C. DRYDEN, vice president, Traffic, Georgia Highway Express, Inc.: [1] Today, the common carrier industry, both truck and rail, stands as a no-growth group—at least I can speak positively for the trucking industry. In the last few years there has been no growth other than that brought about by rate increases and inflation. As I interpret the situation, since the railroads have been losing market share for years the question concerns not truck freight or rail freight but common carrier freight. But common ownership can move this traffic only back and forth between the common carrier modes, if it moves at all.

Now, when everybody is starving and there appear to be no other resources, we fall back on common ownership. It reminds me of the picture of the little fish swimming along with his mouth open, followed by a bigger fish with his mouth open, followed by a still bigger fish with his mouth open. Trucking is the little fish, railroads are the bigger fish, and private carriage is the biggest fish of all. While we are busy eating each other's lunches, private carriage is eating both our lunches.

Common ownership is cannibalistic; it serves no good purpose for common carriage and should therefore be forgotten. I think a great many railroads have no desire for common ownership. Those that are for common ownership are not interested in creating truck lines to serve the areas that their railroads already serve, since many of them can already do this. The basic thrust behind common ownership is from railroads that want to go beyond their present territory into the territory of another railroad, thus becoming intramodal cannibals. I found in my dealings with the railroads that the only thing they hate worse than trucks is each other.

What's the big deal about common ownership? What's the potential? What's the glory road? I don't see any. Some major railroads have major truck lines as their subsidiaries today. These truck lines are run predominantly as entirely separate profit centers and have not been particularly successful. I do not mean that they are not good truck lines; they are. But they have not obtained a major share of the market nor are they outstandingly profitable. While some are tied to key-point restrictions, others operate purely as common carriers.

The issue, then, is not whether common ownership would move freight over two different modes. It does not appear to work that way. Generally, all-truck is more competitive, particularly in the shorter

[1] Mr. Dryden's remarks are from a paper prepared by Dillon Winship, Jr., president, Georgia Highway Express, Inc., and former chairman, American Trucking Associations, who was unable to attend the seminar.

77

haul, than rail. Therefore, when the railroad has a truck line or truck authority, it usually runs it like a truck line. The revenue of all the railroad-owned truck lines in the United States together would be a drop in the bucket, however, compared with the revenue of all the railroads. If a truck and a train are side by side in competition at equivalent rates, the truck is going to haul the freight every time, because it will practically always give better service on truckload traffic. The only way the rails can attract the traffic necessary to be successful intermodally with common ownership would be to cut rates, thus giving two levels of service at two levels of cost, which is not altogether a bad idea, if the railroads can afford to reduce their prices.

If the profitable railroad reduced its prices and ate the lunch of the unprofitable railroads that could not afford to reduce rates, the free enterprise boys would all jump up and shout "How wonderful!" But the result would be oligopoly, and then all the antitrust boys would jump up and shout "How wonderful!" The free enterprise boys would merely have moved the regulations from one band of bureaucrats to another.

Only two things are going to move freight from private carriage to railroads: service and rates. Theoretically, both those goals can be met by the railroads without benefit of common ownership. Why hasn't intermodalism grown? Again, in the majority of cases, the answer lies not in rates but in service. I recently spoke to a major motor carrier who used to ship 350 pigs a week by railroad, but he stopped because rail service simply could not compete with all-truck service.

The second thing that has prevented the growth of intermodal transportation is the Teamsters' restriction on the use of Plan V service by regulated motor carriers.[2] Under this restriction a motor carrier has to run its board (or use all its drivers) before it can put any freight on the railroad. Why would a railroad want to invest in equipment and give service to an industry that is going to use it only for the overflow periods when the economy is good? When the economy is bad, the railroad would be left high and dry with all the equipment that was purchased to handle the movement during the peak period. Consequently, the railroads are not eager to do business with the regulated common carriers. In fact, the only reason they got involved with Georgia Highway was that a restriction in our certificate forced us to use the railroads. Therefore, they knew that we would use them year-round to the extent of our ability.

---

[2] Plan V is one of the basic ICC-approved plans regulating piggyback service. It deals with any combination of motor-rail movement. Rates charged may be either rail or motor. The participating carriers conclude an interchange agreement for movement of the trailer and agree to the division of revenues. See the appendix to this volume for a description of the various piggyback plans.

With a stagnant industry and, consequently, a stagnant labor situation, it would seem wise to reconsider the restrictions that simply result in more private carriage. If the restrictions were removed, it would at least be possible to have growth in short-haul trucking in conjunction with the railroads. In combination, these two could certainly be more competitive to private carriage than they are today.

The last major barrier to the growth of intermodal transportation in lieu of common ownership is that railroads inherently distrust truck lines and truck lines inherently distrust railroads, with some obvious historical justification. Not wanting to be the overflow carrier for the truck lines, the railroads simply do not give Plan V concurrences to the truck lines, and I do not blame them, given the labor situation. But there is never going to be intermodal freight unless the railroads give carriers concurrences. The railroads have been very concerned that giving concurrences to the common carrier truck lines might adversely affect one of their major shippers, the freight forwarders. The trucking industry has for years pushed for mandatory through routes and joint rates. Ultimately, a voluntary rather than a legislative agreement to do this would be in the best interest of the regulated common carrier industry.

I happen to believe that what the rails do best is pull a lot of freight from key point to key point. They are much better off doing a great deal of business with many different carriers at either end of the key point, leaving themselves open to serve all equally, than they would be by offering competitive through truck service. The railroads would end up hauling only the freight that they could generate from main point to main point, since the other truck lines obviously would not give their freight to a competitor who serves their territory nose-to-nose. Although railroads might pick up some more freight through common ownership, they would lose the ability to grow through intermodalism that should result in the absence of common ownership.

I have talked about common ownership, but I have not yet responded to the question: Would carriers form intermodal companies if the barriers were removed? Yes, I think they would. There were five or so long-haul motor carriers that went into the airfreight forwarding business at the same time that we at Georgia Highway Express and several railroads, including Burlington Northern, also went into the airfreight business. Most of the long-haul truck lines quickly learned their lesson and got out. It took us about three years of slow, consistent hard work and losses to turn our operation around so that it has become profitable.

The people at Burlington Northern, with its tremendous economic power, said, "We're going to make it work," and they went out and got market share. They invested millions of dollars and lost a tremendous amount, but they did turn it around and became a major power in the airfreight forwarding business. This is an example of the economic power of major corporations versus that of small corporations. The railroads can lose money ad infinitum until they gain market share in a particular intermodal industry; they can afford to do it. Most of the smaller carriers cannot afford to lose money and are certainly not going to buy a railroad.

Today, practically anybody can get an airfreight forwarder's license. A year from today,[3] anybody can go into the air cargo business, and I do not know why they should not. Flying Tiger and others want to get into the trucking business in order to feed their airlines. Why should the truck lines not get into the air cargo business? I think some of this will take place, but I am not qualified to discuss whether barge lines and pipelines and railroads should get into common ownership. I know there are some barge holding companies that today own truck lines.

As I see it, common ownership is basically a cannibalistic enterprise. Nothing is to be gained by anybody if it is permitted. The people who are encouraging common ownership will be disappointed because it will not create intermodalism. It will merely create separate transportation companies under a common holding corporation. This is not intermodalism. Our airfreight forwarder is entirely separate from our common carrier truck line, except in some of the administrative functions. The railroads usually run their truck lines entirely separately from their rail operation, though not always.

The real issue is: Can railroads or other modes—but, in this case, specifically railroads—diversify by buying a truck line? For railroads there are many opportunities for diversification that are probably more profitable than truck lines. Since they are not barred from any form of diversification other than that relating to transportation, their opportunities are boundless. I see no reason why they should be permitted to enter into common ownership, which would create interfraternity cannibalism and provide opportunity for nefarious schemes ultimately leading to oligopolies. I, for one, do not believe in making work for a bunch of antitrust lawyers. Theirs appears to be a bottomless pit of opportunity in any event.

To put the icing on the cake, let us get down to practical politics. The railroads are divided on this issue and are scared to death of each other. The trucking industry is not divided on this issue. It is fundamentally and in principle against common ownership. Now, if the railroads do not want it any more than they do, and if the trucking in-

---

[3] On November 9, 1977, the Federal Aviation Act of 1958 was amended to permit "any citizen" not already carrying air cargo to apply one year later for an all-cargo air service certificate (P.L. 95-163, adding section 418).

dustry is opposed as much as it is, legislation to permit common ownership would have a dubious future. I do not see citizens marching in
the streets, waving banners, and shouting on bullhorns. I see forty
men sitting around a room, most of whom are probably against common ownership, and the only ones who are for it are those with the
economic power to abuse it.

J. ROBERT HARD, vice president, American Commercial Barge Line
Company: I am not going to talk about bulk exemptions or user charges
or the advantages of water compelled rates because that is not our
topic today. I am going to try to stick to the topic and perhaps try
to be a little more practical than philosophical about the questions of
multimodal ownership. Of course, I'll be speaking only to the problems between water carriers and railroads.

First, since we are talking about eliminating barriers, we need
to define what the barriers are. Let me state, flat out, they are few.
The railroads constantly complain about restrictions, but they really
do not have much relation to their problems. Under today's regulatory structure, there is very little that a railroad could not do if it
wanted to. Basically, there are only two restrictions on the ability of
a railroad to get into water carrier operations. The first is that, because
railroads are already regulated by the Interstate Commerce Commission, they have to go to the ICC if they want to acquire a regulated
barge line, just as they would to acquire another railroad or a truck
line or expand their operating rights. That is purely a problem of control.

The second restriction is referred to as a Panama Canal Act problem. Not that it has much to do with the Panama Canal, but basically
it restricts the ability of a railroad to engage in the barging business,
whether regulated or unregulated, if that business does or may compete
with that railroad on a single-line basis. The Panama Canal Act is
thus concerned only with a railroad's having parallel operations that
include both water and rail carriage.

That's it. That's all there is to it.

As for the regulatory status of the barging industry, probably not
more than 10 to 15 percent of the freight that moves on the waterways of this country is regulated. Just because we at American Commercial Barge Line have an operating certificate does not mean that
everything we move is regulated. In our case, somewhere between 10
and 15 percent of the freight is regulated; for some other barge lines,
it may range as high as 40 to 50 percent. Freight on Ohio Barge Line,
which is U.S. Steel's own private operation, operating as a contract
carrier, is virtually 100 percent regulated. Obviously, no railroad is
going to acquire Ohio Barge Line. And no railroad wants any water

carrier for its regulated traffic because that traffic is mainly complementary to what the railroads now carry. It often produces revenue for them. What do the railroads really want? I think they want end-to-end matches.

Out of the total freight that the water carriers haul, probably not more than 10 to 15 percent—maybe a little more, depending on the water carrier and on the railroad—is even susceptible to diversion to a railroad. Water carriers are set up to handle, for example, bauxite or other ores that come into the New Orleans area and move up the river to the steel and aluminum mills; or they carry coal to the steel mills and utilities that are located along the rivers. There is no substantial risk of diversion in these cases. The only way water carriers could get hurt would be if the competitive situation changed to such a great degree that they were driven off the rivers.

If a railroad wants to haul coal on the rivers there is absolutely no problem, unless the water carrier does or may compete with the railroad and thus comes under the Panama Canal Act. Southern Railway won a decision in a case that was litigated extensively and that involved the question of whether it did or might compete with a water carrier. The ICC decided that there was no barrier to Southern Railway's getting into that business. If the business is not regulated it does not come under the control of the ICC, and if it is not parallel business there is no restriction to entry.

Another example is the case of my own company, American Commercial Barge Line, which works very closely with the Burlington Northern. We are in the process of developing a large coal terminal in St. Louis, and we will take coal from there down the Mississippi to our customers in the Louisiana area. We plan to move probably 20 to 30 million tons a year of this coal that Burlington brings out of the western coal fields. If Burlington wanted to barge that coal to Louisiana itself there is absolutely no restriction on its doing so. The point I want to make is: Why are we concerned about removing barriers if the barriers are not there? Are we perhaps tilting at windmills that are not even there?

One other point I'd like to make is that water carriers could not buy a railroad and would not be interested in doing so. Nor do they have economic leverage on the rivers to capture the railroad business. It just does not work that way. Our concern is that it would work just the other way. The railroads have a captive business. I speak only of railroads because there is little intermodal activity between truckers and barge lines. Basically, the freight we handle is incompatible in volume and type with trucks. We are, however, enormously concerned that the railroads will exert tremendous economic leverage on the captive business any time they decide to move into the river business, as Burlington could have done through St. Louis, if it had wanted to, because it controls the rail rate from Wyoming to St. Louis. All we have is our little share of the market, and we have to make money on that. If the entry of rails or any other group having a superior economic advantage is permitted to any greater degree, attention has to be given to developing antitrust-type sanctions against abuse of their economic power. Water carriers must remain free from the stifling effect of antitrust-exempt rate bureaus and the other kinds of regulations that govern the movement of freight on land.

In summary, my reaction to a proposal to eliminate the minimal barriers that exist would probably be: Why do that until we have tried what we have? Why not see if we can work together? Why do the railroads not get into water carrier operations now, since they have the ability to do so? But, if they do, we need substantial antitrust safeguards.

MR. BARNUM: Would either Jim Amoss or Charles Hiltzheimer speak for a segment of the transportation industry that has not yet had a chance to be heard? Would they like to offer any observations on the question as to what would happen if the barriers, such as they are, were eliminated? Is there any interest on the part of the ocean carriers to expand their activities into other forms of inland or surface transportation? Can I ask you first to give us your thoughts on that, Mr. Hiltzheimer?

CHARLES I. HILTZHEIMER, chairman and chief executive officer, Sea-Land Service, Inc.: I would be glad to comment on behalf of the ocean carriers. It is my view that there probably would not be any major interest in going into ownership of other modes of transportation. In fact, there are no real barriers in international commerce to doing that today. As an example, American Export Lines attempted to be multimodal in a true sense, but their experiment in moving into various other modes and ownership in addition to water carriage recently ended in bankruptcy.

Sea-Land is a multimodal carrier of a sort. We own intrastate trucking rights in Alaska and therefore have a continuous operation in domestic trade by sea and inland truck delivery throughout the state. But we would prefer to do business with various carriers at each end, rather than to control, operate, and own our own delivery and pickup system. There are some disadvantages. If Sea-Land owned a railroad, for example, we would have to make sure that the railroad could serve all our needs throughout the United States because other railroads probably would not cooperate with us if we were in competition with them. There are no real barriers in international commerce today to an ocean carrier's owning and operating other modes, but I see little real economic advantage to the company or the consumer in trying to corral the various inland modes and marry them with ocean transportation.

Another example is Transway International, which emphasizes in its advertising that it is a multimodal company. It does own various modes of transportation, but there is little evidence that they connect with each other or that they are really used together. Transway is in carloading and container manufacture, ocean transportation, airfreight forwarding, and so on. I see no evidence that its ownership of these various entities is beneficial to the total movement of its cargo or the total charter of its company, whatever that might be. Transway does not seem to be designed to take any particular advantage of the fact that it is in these different modes.

On behalf of ocean carriers, and particularly my own company, Sea-Land, I do not see any real advantage that would make us want to go out and buy a railroad or own a number of truck lines in the United States or overseas at this time.

MR. BARNUM: Kenneth McLaughlin, who is president of Universal Carloading, one of Transway's large profit centers, is here today. Would you make a remark or two in response to Mr. Hiltzheimer?

KENNETH MCLAUGHLIN, president, Universal Carloading & Distributing Co., Inc.: The basic reason Transway is unable to put all these pieces together is that regulations prohibit it. The forwarding divisions cannot enter into joint rates with the water divisions. The freight forwarding divisions cannot enter into contracts—other than 409 [4] or local contracts—with the trucking divisions. But we're ready and willing to go when Washington lets us.

MR. BARNUM: But is Mr. Hiltzheimer's observation accurate concerning the coordination of the various modes within Transway?

MR. MCLAUGHLIN: The modes operate individually, and though we talk a lot about what we would like, we are able to do very little toward true intermodal usage of what we own because of the regulatory situation.

MR. BARNUM: Mr. Amoss, would you like to supplement this discussion with your own remarks?

W. J. AMOSS, president, Lykes Bros. Steamship Co., Inc.: First, I would like to say, as a competitor to Sea-Land, that I can think of a number of railroads that I would like to see them acquire.

We seem to be interchanging the words "multimodal" and "intermodal" as we talk here today. While I believe we are really talking

---

[4] Section 409 of the Interstate Commerce Act, 49 U.S.C. § 1009.

about multimodal ownership, intermodal keeps creeping in. That is interesting to me because the real growth of intermodal transportation started with ocean carriers, which developed a container that transposes between the various modes of freight. Other developments on the water side have produced barges that are intermodal to the integrated towage systems on both our inland waterways and our intercoastal system. I think it is fair to say that the deep-sea transportation sector to which Mr. Hiltzheimer and I belong has shown tremendous leadership in intermodal development, which has in turn raised the question of multimodal ownership. The papers prepared for this conference, however, do not pay much attention to international water transportation in the discussion of multimodal ownership.

One concern I have as a representative of an international carrier is with multimodal ownership between, say, a railroad and a water carrier. I would hope that Ben Biaggini's characterization of that combination as a profit center operation would be correct and that ownership of a number of corporations would not give rise to a "distribution philosophy" whereby the interests of one transportation endeavor would be submerged to the benefit of another. I think there should be protection against such a course.

Integration of American-flag (and U.S.-owned) ocean transportation companies into multimodal conglomerates presents some special problems that require careful consideration. In our international commerce now are a number of independent American-flag international carriers and a majority of foreign-owned carriers, including conglomerate foreign carriers, democratic state-owned, socialist state-owned, and communist country fleets. Obviously this diversity poses an array of serious problems that underlie the whole question of multimodal operations on an international scale.

Yet, I feel that there is some advantage to be gained.

I was particularly pleased to see the paper that Paul Hall submitted, in which he expresses the hope that multimodal ownership will extend to the international field, because I believe that great economies can be made. If the container or the barge that moves international freight in domestic commerce is owned by the ocean carrier, then the capital investment in those physical assets has come largely from the ocean carrier side. I think large economies can be made through a more even sharing of those assets that move from mode to mode. I also agree with Mr. Hall's paper that recognition of multimodal ownership of transportation could result in the development of a more aware national transportation policy, extending beyond our own borders in ocean transportation as it has somewhat in air transportation.

I would say, on balance, that I would like to see the subject continue to be developed and discussed, and I hope that ultimately we can devise an approach that will recognize all the advantages and all the problems to be dealt with.

MR. BARNUM: Bob Schaefer from Emery Air Freight is the only representative from the air cargo community here, because at the last moment Wayne Hoffman of Flying Tiger was prevented from coming. Do you want to add a word as to what might happen in the air cargo sector if the existing barriers to multimodal ownership were eliminated? Would more air cargo and surface freight and water freight operations be collected in holding companies? Is that a likelihood from your vantage point?

A. ROBERT SCHAEFER, director of marketing, Emery Distribution Systems, Inc.: Emery Air Freight owns a series of subsidiaries that used to be called D. C. Andrews as a freight forwarder and is now renamed Emery Ocean Freight. We are a multimodal company in the sense that we provide to our shippers any number of modes of transportation today, including carloading for export and non-vessel-owning common carriage, which combine to provide through container movements.

We do split our profit and loss centers and find that it is not only to our corporate advantage but also to our shippers' advantage because we can work together with our parent organization, Emery Air Freight, for instance, to construct rates that are priced to meet certain shipper needs. I also share Ken McLaughlin's thought that it is tough, under ICC regulations, to construct the kinds of through rates we would like to see our shipping public enjoy.

As Harvey Romoff has commented in his paper,[5] there are opportunities in Canada for multimodal moves of airfreight in combination with sea freight. In fact, some of the roll-on, roll-off vessels that sail to the Middle East out of the United Kingdom carry airfreight because of airport congestion in the Middle East. It turns out to be faster to move the airfreight via these high-speed ships with quick discharge capability than to face airport congestion. Although it will be some time before we see true multimodalism occur, it is coming, and I think Emery Air Freight's concept is that multimodalism will be an asset to the shipping community.

MR. BARNUM: Both Fred Rooney and Bud Shuster are going to have to leave soon, and I want to give them an opportunity now to ask any questions of the speakers that have already addressed this first question, or to make any comments that they might like.

CONGRESSMAN FRED B. ROONEY, chairman, House Subcommittee on Transportation and Commerce: I think this symposium will give us a

---

[5] See "Multimodal Ownership in Transportation: A Canadian Perspective," in Part I of this volume.

very valuable insight into how the industry feels about intermodal ownership. The discussion here this morning points up the great problem we have in Congress, and that is not having one transportation committee to deal with all modes of transportation. We are talking today about barge lines, about truckers, about trans-Atlantic shipments, about railroads. Once the National Transportation Policy Study Commission comes up with some kind of a solution to all the problems of transportation, I hope that Congress, in its wisdom, will have one committee dealing with this problem.

Two of the greatest problems in this country today are energy and transportation. I sometimes think we are the only first-rate nation in the world with a second-rate transportation system. We have to do something about it, and seminars and symposiums such as this will go a long way in helping Chairman Shuster and myself decide how Congress will react to the problem.

MR. BARNUM: The ball is in your court, Bud. Have you got the answer up your sleeve?

CONGRESSMAN BUD SHUSTER, ranking minority member, House Subcommittee on Surface Transportation, and chairman, National Transportation Policy Study Commission: I'm afraid not. But the commission certainly is wrestling with issues like this, and we view this symposium as a very worthwhile effort.

I wonder if before I got here the inherent economic benefits of vertical integration were touched on. It seems to me that thread ought to be followed throughout this discussion here today. We should investigate whether the theoretical economic benefits of vertical integration fit the reality of multimodal ownership. I view it as fundamental and very basic, and I hope that it would be considered as part of the whole free market approach in America.

MR. BIAGGINI: We see here in these differing viewpoints what happens as a result of regulation of transportation in the first place. Regulation to meet a particular problem or to handle a particular segment of the business gives rise to an organization or an entity either to handle that part of the business or to take advantage of the aberration in the total transportation picture that caused the regulation in the first place. These entities grow and the aberrations grow, and finally the people who are running these operations get a vested interest—it does not take long to get a vested interest in some part of transportation—and then those people are up on Capitol Hill looking for protection. They took advantage of a situation in the first place, but later on they want protection from all the others who are looking for special advantages. The people sitting around this table who are pretty well satisfied with their situation right now will be asking Congress for more protection ten or fifteen years from now.

It seems to me that we need to be looking for a gradual relaxation of regulation in transportation. I am all for the common carrier system, and I think we have a fine one in this country. Certainly there should be transportation generally available for people who have goods to move and for people who want to travel on a common carrier. (Before we get into a big discussion about the railroad passenger business, however, I would like to say that it has probably been outmoded by technology in most places.) But the more we can rely on the principles of the free market system—which basically is what has made this country a great industrial power and a great economic power—and the more we can let people in the transportation business do whatever they are able to do without a large body of regulations, the better off the country is going to be. It is going to take time, but if we don't get started pretty quick we are never going to get there.

I envy Mr. Hard's position. He is in a multimodal company right now. He has truck lines, barge lines, and pipelines, and he could very well afford a railroad, but he thinks the railroad business is so unattractive he does not want to get into it. He sees the boot heel of regulation on the neck of the railroads, and he cannot see any way to make any money out of railroads as he can out of the barge line and the pipeline and the highly profitable business of hauling automobiles. We are in a great cooperative endeavor with him in that regard.

I think these deliberations this morning will point in one direction: We are going to have to try to turn this transportation business toward less regulation rather than more.

MR. HARD: I think those are valid comments. There is a great degree of intermodal ownership in our economy now. For instance, in my company, American Commercial Barge Line, we do have a natural gas pipeline, but it produces not one cent of revenue for barging or for trucking. We have a large common carrier motor carrier, but I do not know of one pound of freight that has ever interchanged between the motor carrier and the barge line. We have a rather large automobile hauling business. It is competitive with the railroads and is getting more competitive because of the railroads' damage problems and so on. It does not produce one pound of freight for the barge lines.

To go back to what I was saying earlier, it is not common ownership that we are afraid of—we could have that now. Practically any railroad could get into any end-to-end barge line operation that they want to today. We are concerned about the economic leverage that railroads have because of the captive nature of their traffic.

MR. BARNUM: I would like to ask Ben Biaggini one question. You mentioned that if it were easier for railroads to acquire motor carriers, you would envision end-to-end acquisitions, taking railroads into new geographical markets beyond the limits of their existing markets. Would greater freedom to do that deter your interest in extending your geographical markets by acquiring other railroads, which in turn might frustrate the concept of the longer haul continental railroad?

MR. BIAGGINI: I don't think so. It seems to me that moving ahead in all directions in transportation would be worthwhile. One of the great problems of the railroad industry has been the lack of its ability to grow. It is almost impossible to expand into new markets because of the geographical nature of the business and its corporate segmentation.

Any industrial company can go into new markets or develop new products, but, as Dillon Winship's paper points out,[6] we are in the business of furnishing transportation. To get economies of scale—and I think there are economies of scale in transportation—we grow by acquisition. That is what the transcontinental motor carriers have done—Consolidated Freightway, and Navajo, and PIE [Pacific Intermountain Express], and so forth—and I think those are successful, well-run companies. They suffer from the same burden of regulation that the railroads do, but I digress a bit from your question.

I would think that a transcontinental railroad company would also want to be a transcontinental trucking company so that it would have the advantage of being able to render other services complementary to its basic business, such as the pickup and delivery of piggyback containers and things of that sort. Our trucking company, however, does not pick up and deliver all our piggyback trailers or all the containers. There are literally dozens of truck lines that come into the terminals and pick up the trailer and containers. Freight forwarders do most of their own pickup and delivery. A lot of private carriage does most of its own pickup and delivery now. There is a whole series of different plans for piggybacking. But I think it is beneficial to have at least the ability to be in these other kinds of business so that we know what the problems and the opportunities are. As we learn more about the other fellow's business we are able to do a better job for ourselves.

MR. BARNUM: Mr. Jones, we have not heard from a pipeline operator, except as an ancillary business of some of the other speakers. Are there any comments you would like to make in response to this first question?

VERNON T. JONES, president, Williams Pipeline Company: Undoubtedly there would be multimodal companies developed further, although they already exist in a great many areas. I think that regulatory inhibitions are one of the greatest problems we face when we try to expand into

---

[6] See the remarks of Robert C. Dryden, above.

other transportation and transportation-related businesses. Our own particular business right now is in somewhat of a regulatory vacuum since we have just had a change of agency. Some very crucial questions are without answers and have been for some time. But, basically, I think that the opportunities we are interested in exist for us today without any significant changes.

MR. BARNUM: Without going into other modes of transportation?

MR. JONES: Yes, at least without going beyond what we are allowed to do under the existing statutes.

JOHN J. TERRY, group vice president, Land Transportation, IU International Management Corporation: I was impressed by Paul Roberts' paper because it shed some light on one of the intermodal ownership areas, the rail-truck. I do not care whether they let the railroads buy truck lines, but I was struck by the table that shows the piggyback eligible freight that moves between a number of points and by the map that shows the number of equivalent trailer loads per day of piggyback eligible traffic.[7] For a railroad to have a viable piggyback service to those city pairs, it would have to get an enormous share of the market—30 or 40 percent of the total traffic moving—and there is no way that a railroad that owned a truck line could ever get that kind of market share. The only reasonable chance of reaching that market share is by working with rather than against the other modes. If the railroad owns a motor carrier that operates from, say, Los Angeles to Houston, competing motor carriers are not going to put their trailers on that train, and as a result the market share needed for profitable operation would be unattainable. Roberts' paper indicates to me that rail-truck intermodal ownership offers little for the public interest. It is almost proven by his intercity freight flow data plus the rail affiliates' operating results.

The operating results of rail-owned motor carriers are disappointing and their growth is insignificant; if there were anything to be gained from intermodal ownership, the results would be better. I guess a good reason to allow intermodal ownership is to see if it will provide some help, but it seems pretty clear to me that it will not.

MR. BIAGGINI: I have to respond to that comment about the rail-owned trucking lines. The performance of the rail-owned trucking lines has been marginal at best simply because of the restrictions—the prior-and-subsequent-rail-haul and the key-point restrictions. It is hard to visualize the situation, but, for instance, when a driver for a rail-trucking line goes to a shipper's dock and looks over a pile of freight he may have to say, "I can take those two cartons but not the other five." That

---

[7] See Table 2 and Figure 8 in "Consolidation: Key to Multimodal Freight Transportation" in Part I above.

shipper will not call that trucker often, except to move those other two cartons or the "bird cages" and similar things that the highly selective common carrier trucking industry is not going to solicit under any circumstances.

If we removed the various artificial restrictions that were made to protect the trucking industry back in 1935 after the Motor Carrier Act, I think that the people who manage the railroad-owned trucking lines could manage them just as well as anybody else when given a fair shake in the competitive market. The test will be what happens in the next four or five years now that ICC policy seems to be more liberal with respect to eliminating those restrictions.

HAROLD M. SHAY, president, Shay's Service, Inc.: I am of the sparrow species of bird life. There are literally thousands and thousands of us as opposed to the lone eagles, and something is being overlooked here. I know what the question is, but I do not know the problem. Intermodalism is our life. Bob Dryden addressed this in bringing us Dillon Winship's remarks. Shay's Service has somewhat the same type of operation as Georgia Highway Express, but we are truly short-haul carriers, like about 15,000 others. The drivers for a short-haul carrier return to their base of operation every day. Whether the tour of duty is within the commercial zone or far out, the driver must get back to base every day under the regulations which govern the operation. I am referring to areas up to 200 miles from the point of interchange. Whenever I talk to other intermodal carriers, however, I find that they are short-haul carriers too. I have had Consolidated Freightway's Gene West tell me that they are a short-haul carrier—but they have one-tenth of one-half percent of their short-haul business in Montana because the ICC mandated that they serve the point. We are really short-haul carriers and suffer no small amount in that: "We don't get no respect."

I have to speak only of the rail-truck relationship because that is the only area about which I feel at all knowledgeable. Common ownership would not enhance intermodalism; it would deter it. Somebody—I don't recall who, but I think it was Mr. Terry—just said that by no stretch of the imagination would a motor carrier give its competitor freight to haul.

Intermodalism in the short-haul area and in rural America—and I think this is being overlooked—has to have a mix of traffic. When our vehicles go into the country on a 150-mile run, we may have a mix of freight from Emery Air Freight, Flying Tiger, United Air Lines, and Sea-Land. In any given period we have interline traffic from possibly 100 motor carriers. We also have direct traffic within the state, and this

local traffic is often overlooked. We usually address the problem to interstate traffic, but that is only a part of it.

I feel a bit uncomfortable after hearing the Honorable Fred
Rooney remark that we have a second-class transportation system. The
trucking industry is well, and our own demands on ourselves continue
to make us healthy or we disappear; yet service does not suffer. That
cannot be the case with the rails or even with airlines, but if one of the
kids gets sick I see no reason to operate on his brother.

I am terribly concerned about common ownership. There is no
question it may help the stockholder of a particular company, but I
don't think that is our sole purpose—not that I am naive enough to
think we are in the business to serve the public, paying no attention to
the bottom line. Of course we are interested in profit. To sum up my
position—though we could spend the whole day discussing the advantages and disadvantages of intermodalism between truck and rail—
I see no way for a single entity to take over the local and short-haul
carrier, which is the guts of a transportation system that takes care of
rural and urban America. It would be one of the biggest mistakes that
we could make. I don't know how many people here have been involved
in picking up rail trailers in a yard. I may oversimplify line-haul operations, but I don't see much trouble from point of takeoff to touchdown.
The trouble comes after the freight gets in the airport and we try to
stow it in the belly of a plane or find a trailer in Conrail's yard in
Buffalo. (We really need a detective!) Then if the wheels are round,
we pull it.

What is proposed to take care of this multitude of problems?
Mr. Roberts's paper—which I read three times—asked: Why don't we
give intermodal ownership a go? That really precipitated a thought:
it is a little like throwing the baby out with the bath water. Before any
action is taken—and I know the wheels grind slowly here in Washington—we should have a great deal of dialogue, such as we are having
today; and there should be an opportunity, such as this day will not
afford, to set forth the reasons that we think common ownership and
intermodal ownership would be a deterrent and would be harmful to
the shipping public.

CONGRESSMAN ROONEY: I might say, Mr. Shay, that I was not indicting
the trucking industry. I think the trucking industry in this country today
is a viable industry—and it should be, because the American taxpayer
has put billions of dollars into building highways for trucks to operate
on. I know that trucks pay a user fee, but I am concerned that the
railroads in this country make less than 2 percent annually on their investment. I am concerned that the railroads in the Midwest are going

bankrupt—two of them are bankrupt at present, and the Department of Transportation is doing absolutely nothing about it.

I am concerned about the East. Conrail is losing considerable amounts and is asking for another $1.3 billion in federal financing. How long can the American taxpayer face this problem? I am concerned that a Middle Eastern country wanted to take over the ownership of an airline in this country. I am concerned about the airlines, and I think we have a very serious problem with our national transportation system. I think this symposium will help bring about a salvation of the transportation system in this country.

MR. SHAY: We have an intermodally cooperative type of operation that we believe, and can demonstrate, has been very successful in a small area in the country. We are independently owned and would like to stay that way. I believe that a great deal of what is being discussed this morning can be brought about by a greater degree of cooperation between the modes—joint routes and rates—rather than by common ownership. Perhaps cooperation needs to be given more emphasis than common ownership. With cooperation, each mode is able to do what— at least on the surface—it is best equipped and qualified to do, independent of others. The modes can cooperate with each other to work out individual problems. But with common ownership, there is no place to go.

CONGRESSMAN SHUSTER: I would like to piggyback on what Chairman Rooney had to say. I certainly subscribe to the points he made about the taxpayers' spending millions of dollars to provide highways for trucks. As a member of Congress who represents a large railroad district, Altoona, Pennsylvania, it pains me to recognize that about 47 percent of all the money paid into the Highway Trust Fund is put there by the truckers, even though they represent about 17 percent of the traffic on the highway. As a point of interest, the National Transportation Policy Study Commission is developing a policy to ensure that each user of our nation's highways—and indeed of our whole transportation network—pays a fair share.

MR. SHAY: Just one more minute in response because I do not want my statement misconstrued. Chairman Rooney, I share your sentiments and I have the same concern, being a taxpayer, in addition to being a truckman.

For four years I have co-chaired with an individual from the railroad industry a liaison committee between the short-haul conference of the American Trucking Associations and the National Railroad Piggyback Association. We have almost begged to get a dialogue going because short-haul carriers have no more allegiance to the line-haul carriers than we do to railroads or to airlines. That comes as a surprise. I think that even our regulatory agencies ignore this. I am sorry that Mr. Fitzsimmons isn't here because I would like to have him hear me say that they have not recognized the problem either.

My concluding point is this: We are, in our segment of the industry, the answer to true intermodalism because we can perform it for all. As Bob Dryden has said, if we are going to cannibalize the industry, something is going to wind up as a skeleton. We cannot be a standby to rural America to take care of what somebody else cannot handle or elects not to handle. I certainly share your concern about our railroad system and I am all for it. I just wish they would unlock the door and look on us as a different segment. We are not the trucking that they dislike so much, according to Dillon Winship's comments.[8]

---

[8] Following the conference, Mr. Shay supplemented his remarks as follows:

"If we are truly desirous of having a viable intermodal transportation service, best for the shipping public and best for the investor, then in my opinion it should not be under common ownership.

"The local and short-haul carrier is a very large group of carriers, estimated to be 10,000 to 15,000 in number, many from the early days of truck transportation, that for one reason or another did not grow and expand vertically with the industry. This is not to say that this group of carriers is less efficient. Quite the contrary, it is the most efficient class of carrier of all, generally recognized by any knowledgeable operating transportation person. The demand for efficiency in the short-haul sector is so great that it offers little attraction to the investor and financial institution.

"Herein lies the problem. All modes want to retain only the portion of traffic that is profitable, leaving the unprofitable to shift for itself, better known as traffic selectivity. It has often been said, 'There is no bad traffic, just bad rates.' By our very existence, the short-haul carrier demonstrates that short-haul traffic can be profitable, while the long-haul carrier, of any mode, readily admits the financial burden of this same traffic.

"Some of the more obvious reasons for the short-haul carrier's operating advantages follow:
1. Mix of traffic from all modes in addition to local traffic moving on the same vehicles. Certainly, competitive line-haul carriers of all modes are not going to share their traffic with their competitors in the A & D [assembly and distribution] areas.
2. Manpower productivity within small family-owned business is reportedly 50 percent greater than that in hourly wage areas of the larger corporations.
3. Service to the shipping public is much more personalized through the local short-haul carrier. He knows the shipper, his problems, and his needs.
4. Better equipment utilization resulting in more efficient fuel uses.
5. While not an economic advantage, certainly the environmental impact is greatly reduced when all vehicles are used to full visible or other limited capacities.

"You may recall my having made the remark that for about four years the Local and Short-Haul Carrier Conference has had a truck/rail liaison committee, willing, ready, and able to assist in the increase of rail/truck intermodalism activities, and the rails are dragging their feet. It is readily recognizable that in the eyes of many rail-oriented people a truck is a truck, and all truckers are competitors. The intramodal activities by truck have been very desirable and natural, but with the advent of the super highway and the expansion of the long-

Second Topic: How would the formation of multimodal companies affect shippers?

MR. BARNUM: All the various transportation operators may be thinking that the shippers have so far been remarkably silent. We have heard from them on numerous other occasions, but today they have held their fire until now. What would the formation of multimodal companies do for the shippers? How do the shippers view the pluses and minuses of multimodal companies? I have asked Bill Smith to lead off the discussion of that subject.

WILLIAM K. SMITH, vice president, General Mills, Inc.: I will be speaking from a background with a company that does a lot of business with transportation companies on the North American continent, very little export, some import. We have transportation arrangements in foreign countries that I know nothing about. Most people look upon General Mills as a so-called big shipper. We do have big shipments. We have shiploads and bargeloads and truckloads and carloads and unit trains and so on. We also have small shipments. We annually ship millions of parcels. We are a fairly major customer with United Parcel and Emery and Federal Express. More than 80 percent of our transportation is common carrier or some form of for-hire carrier. Less than 10 percent is private and less than 10 percent is so-called exempt commodity transportation. We are basically a user of for-hire common carrier transportation, and our small shipment distribution, in quantity and complexity, is greater than our big shipment distribution.

With that background, how does this shipper look upon this subject? I look upon it as a "ho-hum, so what?" kind of subject. That is rather flippant, but I did a little research, and I find that, while many of the shipper organizations are in favor of God, motherhood, flag, and intermodal transportation companies, very few of them have done anything about intermodal transportation. I find that the subject has very low priority, if it has any priority at all.

The National Industrial Traffic League's policy is that common ownership should be permitted, it should avoid the problems of preda-

---

haul motor carriers' scope of operation, the local or short-haul carrier is looking for relief from the dominance of the long-haul motor carrier to serve his long-haul needs. Air and rail are the only alternatives.

"Before we remove the restrictions on common ownership of intermodal systems and further complicate and erode local service, shouldn't these 10,000 or 15,000 established carriers be afforded the opportunity to use their expertise in developing a truly efficient, energy-conserving, environmentally safer intermodal system? I feel strongly that we could follow in the direction that this country has gone in the movement of people unless we continue to offer a comprehensive transportation service to all. Not a very bright picture, and it doesn't need to happen as long as the entrepreneur is left a chance, and the small business can remain self-motivated and competition unstifled."

tory pricing, and it should be in the public interest. The Chamber of Commerce of the United States, of which shippers are a part, also has a policy that common ownership should be permitted. Neither the NIT league nor the Chamber of Commerce, to my knowledge, has done anything about it.

The Transportation Association of America, of which shippers are a part, has no policy on intermodal transportation companies, probably because not all parts of TAA are in agreement on the subject. I am sure the railroad segment of TAA, as Mr. Biaggini has pointed out, would support an intermodal multimodal transportation company policy, since the railroad industry officially supported "total transportation companies" in their ASTRO prospectus.[9] But in 1975 the railroads went to President Ford with their problems, and they did not talk to him about intermodal transportation companies, nor have I seen the concept on the list of thirteen needs that they now have before the government.

Shippers have some input into such things as the Committee on Transportation of the National Academy of Engineering, which does some contract work for the secretary of transportation on policy development. That group says we ought to study intermodal transportation and multimodal transportation companies as ways of increasing productivity. Secretary of Transportation Coleman in 1975 put out a "Statement of National Transportation Policy," but he was not specific on the subject of multimodal transportation companies. Just before leaving office in January 1977, he put out a projection called "National Transportation Trends and Choices," and he said, "It is believed that constructive economic regulatory changes should permit multimodal ownership and operation for improved service."

I have looked at other groups regarding multimodal companies, and I have come up with about the same thing. Many of them have a policy, but nothing has been done. Quite a few shippers have been interested in less regulation in recent years, but I am not sure that many shippers have read Ann Friedlaender's book, *The Dilemma of Freight Transport Regulation,*[10] in which she suggests that the multimodal transportation company might be a useful device that would bring about less regulation without regulatory change.

Today I say, "Ho-hum, so what?" In 1969 I made a speech in which I was all for intermodal transportation companies. Nontransportation companies, such as General Mills, have a degree of freedom to diversify into various nontransportation fields and also into transportation fields. I believed a for-hire transportation company should have a similar degree of freedom, modified by the public interest qualification.

---

[9] A report on the railroad industry prepared by America's Sound Transportation Review Organization (ASTRO) of the Association of American Railroads.
[10] (Washington, D.C.: Brookings Institution, 1969).

I still believe that. In 1969 I said, "I anticipate that the long-range effect on General Mills of such freedom for transportation companies would be more beneficial than harmful." Today I doubt that there would be any benefit to General Mills, and again I say I look upon intermodal transportation as a "ho-hum, so what?" subject.

My thinking began to change in 1970 when the Transportation Association of America put out a questionnaire on the subject. The more I thought about it in answering that questionnaire, the more I began to see that there are many aspects of intermodal or multimodal transportation companies that do not have any application to the shipper because there is more than one shipper. Very few things that move from origin to consumption involve only one shipper. Even where such moves do involve only one shipper, one that can make a decision as to the various modes, that shipper probably has its own transportation company, as does U.S. Steel, which is a multimodal transportation company.

I went through some examples. I played around with iron ore. I know a little about that because iron ore comes out of Minnesota. I looked at coal. I know a little about that because a lot of the coal moving in from Montana and Wyoming either comes into Minnesota or is transferred from unit trains in Minnesota to barges on the Mississippi River to go elsewhere. Because coal is a lively subject, I have become informed on it. I looked at grain, which I know something about—though not as much as Jim Springrose—and decided I really did not see what intermodal companies would do to help or to hinder the shipper in those various areas. Then I looked a bit closer to home, at transportation of food into grocery stores, which is a big item for General Mills.

General Mills does not transport groceries into grocery stores. Grocery stores are a retail outlet, and stock that is manufactured or processed usually flows into a retail outlet from a distributor or wholesaler. A few processed items that go in grocery stores, such as bread, milk, potato chips, or soft drinks, come direct from the processors and not from a distributor. Most of our products are not put in grocery stores by General Mills. They are put there by Safeway or Kroger or Red Owl or whoever owns the grocery store.

Transportation to the store is entirely by truck—usually the distributor's or the processor's private truck. The decision whether to use for-hire truck or private truck is usually made by the distributor or the processor. There is a modal choice for the movement from the manufacturer, such as General Mills, to the distributor, such as Safeway and A & P. The stock can move by rail, by truck, by rail-truck, or various rail-truck combinations. In this case, truck might be the private truck of the manufacturer or processor, or of the distributor, backhauled for him. Pricing practices—how the manufacturer sells to the distributor, how the distributor sells to the retailer—weigh significantly on the choice of mode, if there is a choice, and upon who makes the choice. Labor practices, including those concerning whose truck serves the retail store owned by the distributor, can influence whether the private truck or a for-hire truck is used. The multimodal transportation concept does not appear to me to have any application in the distribution system used for manufactured or processed items going into grocery stores.

Another example is our small shipment distribution. There are many techniques for gathering up small shipments, consolidating them, moving them by some form, breaking up the small shipments, and dispersing them in the area in which freight forwarders and shippers' associations operate. In the distribution of small shipments I think there is some possible application of what we have been talking about this morning.

We operate several kinds of businesses in Canada, but we do not find that the existence there of multimodal transportation companies makes any difference to our distribution, planning, distribution economics, or distribution services. But maybe we don't know enough about Canada. Therefore, I went to some of our competitors, who also have both U.S. and Canadian operations. I talked to their Canadian people— same response. They, too, do not find a difference between the use of multimodal transportation in Canada and the modal approach in the United States. From my experience in this country, where we do not have multimodal transportation companies (with some exceptions, such as Southern Pacific), and from my employer's experience in Canada, where there are such entities, I continue to come forth with a "ho-hum, so what?" attitude toward the subject. I am not ready to seek such companies and probably not ready to oppose them. I am primarily wondering where and how they might be used.

JAMES V. SPRINGROSE, vice president, Transportation, Cargill Incorporated: My experience has been primarily in the movement of dry and liquid cargoes in bulk, and I cannot foresee that multimodal ownership of transportation companies would cause substantial shifts in the distribution patterns. For such cargoes, the use of bags, drums, or other containers has been abandoned in favor of large-volume bulk movements. Although packaging would make bulk commodities more suitable for the modern multimodal concepts, I believe that a return to packaged goods is remote. The economic reasons that caused the initial shift to movement in bulk still apply.

Since that early transition, a very efficient distribution network has been developed, which utilizes the best of all modes of transportation. Although multimodal ownership or service combinations may offer limited opportunities, the probability that they would improve the current bulk distribution system is, in my mind at least, very doubtful. That does not mean that I am against multimodal ownership. If I could see some benefits directly related to the kind of business that Cargill engages in, I would be a very strong advocate of such ownership. My attitude principally is that even though the opportunities are not on the surface and visible, we should not deny the chance to develop those opportunities. I don't think we can restrict the ingenuity of man, and if someone wants to develop multimodal ownership, he should be allowed to do so.

I liken the development of multimodal transportation to that of Cargill Incorporated as a corporation. The agribusiness, our fundamental and primary concern, is comprised of many different phases, but we are not in all of them. Unlike General Mills, we do not distribute and sell a retail brand name because our management really does not know how to do that. The few times we have tried, we have failed and backed off. We content ourselves with managing those phases of our business that we believe we have the capability of managing best.

We are, however, engaged in virtually every phase up to customer items, but without Cargill as a brand name. We distribute millions of dozens of eggs, but they are in Winn-Dixie cartons. We distribute turkeys. Many of the Swift Butterball turkeys are produced by Cargill. We will stuff our birds into anyone's bag—it doesn't matter to us. We do not produce grain except for hybrid seeds. We rely on the efficiencies of the American farmer for the production of grain. But we are in every facet of the marketing and the processing of grain, and we are, in that sense, multimodal.

At the same time there are many small or regional entrepreneurs in specific segments of the business. They are good and strong competitors because they are efficiently run, and they provide a service to the economy. That is essentially the way I visualize multimodal transportation: It, too, comprises many segments, some of which are efficiently run; others are not. I think, however, that it is a matter of speculation whether the efficiency of any one mode or any one company will vary, depending on who owns it. I do not know the final outcome of multimodal ownership, but I can forecast, to some degree, what would happen to the players in the current modal scene in the event that more extensive multimodal ownership were allowed. I believe that the efficient independents would survive and prosper. The marginal ones would probably consolidate, and they would either enhance their efficiency so as to compete or they would become more inefficient. The inefficient in the industry as a whole would simply die away. To my mind, that is the way free enterprise functions best in the general public's interest.

I am no longer frightened by scare words to the effect that the financial might of any mode would enable it to gobble up some other mode, establish a monopoly, and then raise prices. First, my observation is that no one industry, as an industry, has the financial might to undertake such a thing. Second, if the railroads tried to do it—and they are the ones that seem to be pointed to in this regard—and if a monopolistic situation developed and freight rates were too high, it would be easy for others to come back into the trucking and the barging business. To some extent shipping is capital intensive, but it is quite easy to get into private trucking. In fact, the greatest competition to the for-hire carriers today comes from the growth in private carriers.

The threat of the development of monopolies as a result of intermodal ownership has long since passed. The fledglings of the industry that were being protected when the current statutes were written have now matured, and I do not believe they need that protection any more. In sum, I cannot point to any great efficiencies that multimodal ownership would obtain for the kind of business activities that I engage in. We already have the efficiencies of multimodal service that the shipping community has developed. I therefore do not see any great value to multimodal ownership, but, at the same time, I feel that anyone who wants to try should have the opportunity to do so.

CLIFFORD L. WORTH, general traffic manager, Westvaco Company: I am general traffic manager of a large paper company that has a freight bill of about $100 million a year. We have nationwide transportation and distribution—in fact, we have worldwide marketing of our products. My company is high on the list of large customers with an astonishingly long list of American transportation companies.

My original assignment was to comment on how the formation of multimodal companies would affect shippers. But since it is apparent that such companies have been formed already, the gist of my comments ought to be on how elimination of the restrictions that still remain would affect shippers. To keep the discussion in some bounds, I am going to limit it to the effects on carload or truckload or bargeload shippers.

In many industries, there is a concern with all the trade-offs involved in a total distribution effort. For truly effective distribution an organization requires considerable sophistication, particularly in the development of computerization techniques, and considerable dedication on the part of senior management. Not all organizations can be successful in this. In any company, however, the practical, day-to-day concerns with respect to transportation are: its reliability and level of transit performance, availability of equipment, and costs. In costs of transportation I include freight rates, packaging materials, handling, damage, and so on. I will discuss each of these, beginning with transit reliability.

Railroad management openly admits that, for railroads to survive, it is necessary to reduce labor expense as much as possible. The principal techniques are to run fewer trains with each containing more cars, and to automate switching and classification yards. The end result is that a typical repetitive movement of ordinary carload freight may take from four to eleven days. As the number of terminals through which a car moves along its route is increased, the spread will also increase. In short, rail carload service is a practical shipping option only for merchandise going into storage or for inventory. In business transactions with a specific delivery requirement, some other alternative usually must be used, most likely truck. There are specific exceptions, of course. Railroads do offer a degree of transit reliability for large-volume piggyback movements and for unit train movements, but not for the ordinary routine shipping of rail carload freight.

When I speak of truck as the alternative, I am referring to specific categories of trucking, such as irregular-route common carriers, contract carriers, and private truck operations, all of which specialize in truckload transportation. These carriers are routinely in a position to have equipment depart immediately from loading points and proceed directly to destinations on consistent and reliable transit schedules. Barging alternatives, although limited to specific waterway systems and to slow mileage per day, nevertheless offer astonishing transit reliability.

The second item on the list is equipment availability. Of the many activities of an industrial traffic manager, the most irksome, frustrating, and aggravating is arranging a supply of empty rail cars for company use. I can unequivocally state that not one of Westvaco's numerous shipping points—plants, factories, warehouses, or whatever—not one of them receives all the cars it needs all the time. Not one. It is equally and unfortunately true that not even most of the installations receive most of the cars they need most of the time. The alternative again is usually trucking, and it is routinely feasible to make arrangements with the types of truck carrier mentioned earlier that are readily available and will provide a dedicated fleet of trucks and trailers.

The third point concerns costs. In the 1960s truckload freight rates were, for the most part, considerably higher than corresponding rail rates. Since then rail rates have increased much more rapidly than truckload rates. As a result, current truckload rates are less than, the same as, or only slightly higher than the corresponding rail rates. In general, the costs of loading, packaging, and damage are also less for truck shipments than for rail.

Now let me put all this together. Industrial traffic managers are expected to exhibit great ingenuity in taking account of all the factors in these three basic concerns to develop optimum usage of modal alternatives to produce favorable results for their company. Although statistics are not available, I have the impression that most freight moves directly from origin point to destination via a single mode. There are, however, at least these notable exceptions and there may be others: the movement of large tonnage via barge involving prior or later movements by truck or rail; the movement of freight in containers by rail involving prior or later movements by truck; and movement via rail or truck which, for one reason or another, requires a transfer of lading and local cartage delivery at final destination.

The question then becomes: How would shippers be affected if multimodal companies could offer coordinated services under a unified responsibility and at through freight rates? In responding, I envision a company that could offer any one or a combination of rail, barge, and truck, including common carrier, irregular route common carrier, or contract carrier services.

The affirmative effects that come to mind are, first, a desirable relief from having to make separate shipping arrangements with two or more transportation companies for single through movements. Arrangements include providing for empty equipment, issuing and signing bills of lading, arranging for delivery inspection and receipts, receiving and paying freight bills within the legal time limits, resolving loss and damage problems, and negotiating schedules. The shipper would state the constraints as to quantities, pickup and delivery time, and any other element of importance, and the prime carrier would then make available the optimum alternatives of equipment and services to achieve the desired result. This would be an advantage, compared with what a shipper must go through now, researching and making individual arrangements with several separate carriers.

Second, there is a possibility that a through rate—or through freight cost—negotiated with a multimodal company would be more favorable than the sum of the separate dealings with several transportation companies. Transportation pricing is far more an art than a science, and a skilled negotiator, representing a shipper, surely should be able to end up with a better rate from a single counterpart than from several separate entities.

One nuisance in an industrial traffic manager's life is the problem of pinning down responsibility for transit damage in intermodal transportation. Carrier A will claim the damage must have occurred while the shipment was in the possession of carrier B and vice versa. One real advantage of dealing with a single intermodal transportation company would be the ability to sidestep the issue of where liability lies, thereby speeding the appropriate recovery.

A final advantage of dealing with a unified intermodal transportation company would be the opportunity for a shipper to negotiate for improved transit performance and reliability. A fictional situation to illustrate the point might be that of a consistent flow of freight with truck movement in containers from A to B, at which point the containers are placed on flatcars by a local drayage company for movement by rail to point C, where the containers are transferred and moved by barge to D, the final destination. Coordinating and monitoring each portion of these movements would be a monumental task for a shipper. It would be difficult, perhaps even impossible, to work out long-lasting improvements in performance and reliability. If all these services were performed under the aegis of a single intermodal company, however, the whole atmosphere would be different. Each segment would be controllable and negotiable as part of a coordinated whole. There would indeed be ample opportunity for a shipper to develop and implement constructive improvements.

These observations about advantages are all specifically keyed to movements of freight that require more than one mode from origin to destination. Now I want to consider briefly the movement of freight via a single mode, but a movement which would be part of, or controlled by, a multimodal venture. The key advantage in such a situation would be financial power—that is, the resources of a large multimodal company should enable each segment to have better, or perhaps more, equipment than it could justify or finance by itself. And if, in such a circumstance, the particular mode were allowed to operate freely under its own management, the consequences to a shipper could be most favorable.

Under the negative effects of allowing and perhaps encouraging development of intermodal agencies, it would be proper to include, first, an uneasiness—difficult to pin down, but nevertheless real—that a successful multimodal company could grow large enough to dominate and overwhelm competition. I do not know how to expand on this idea, but it is easy to envision a monster transportation company that smaller competitors could not meet or beat.

Second—with a smile to my neighbor who represents the Interstate Commerce Commission—there is the virtual certainty of added regulations by the ICC or kindred agencies. We often hear of the heavy hand of regulation. Despite high-sounding words to the contrary from the ICC and other agencies, it is not easy for a shipper to receive a quick response when one is needed. When emergency operating authority is needed to permit an unusual movement of freight—to keep a plant running, for example—it usually takes several days for the ponderous bureaucracy to react. Meanwhile the crisis will have passed or will have been resolved by some other means.

Similarly, when the problem is one of economics and not operating right, permission for a carrier to make an essential freight rate change quickly also takes at least several days. My personal experience with a long series of searing transportation emergencies underlies my concern with the potential harm of added regulation of a multimodal company. For instance, I can envision rather rigid rules designed to slow down decision-making so as to allow nonintegrated competition ample time to react and protest. I can picture a regulatory umbrella designed to keep the freight charges of a coordinated operation high enough to protect less efficient nonintegrated competition, and so on.

A final and considerable negative effect would be the possibility that the mere bigness of a multimodal company could stifle internal entrepreneurship and innovation. I base this observation on a good many years of experience in dealing with large railroads and small railroads, with large trucking companies and small ones, and with big steamship lines and little ones. In my opinion, the ability of a carrier to react to ideas and to implement change is inversely proportional to its size and the layers of management that must be penetrated. I can readily foresee that, once a multimodal company reached its maturity, rigidity would set in. From that point on, dealing with such an organization would be essentially similar to trying to bring about some novel development in one of the large railroad systems. Such projects are not impossible, but extremely difficult to bring to a successful conclusion. I would predict similar and probably compounded difficulties in attempting to deal with multimodal companies of the future.

None of these affirmative and negative effects that might follow from freeing the creation of multimodal ventures is truly overwhelming. The entire list is almost of secondary importance and, for the most part, the elements are highly speculative. They seem to balance out fairly well. My conclusion is that formation of multimodal companies would not substantially affect carload, truckload, or bargeload shippers. But let me add two observations. The first is a tenet by which I attempt to manage the affairs of my company: Transportation companies are not here for the purpose of moving freight; they are here to make money. And if transportation companies see, in the creation of a multimodal venture, an opportunity for success, let it happen. My second point is that since it is reasonably clear that legislative and regulatory changes are needed to bring this about, do not expect much support or excitement from shippers.

MR. BARNUM: Tom Browne is a shipper, a carrier, and a very good client of some. If you have some observations on the shipping side of your activities at UPS we would be pleased to hear them.

THOMAS W. BROWNE, vice president, United Parcel Service: As a company, we do not have any real feelings about intermodal ownership. But some things seem a little strange. For example, it is much easier for a noncarrier to buy a carrier than it is for another carrier to buy a carrier, and that seems a little strange. Also, for many years the regulators seem to have resisted a coast-to-coast railroad. I do not know whether that would have helped the rail situation, but it might have made the interline rail carriers a little more service conscious.

Clifford Worth hit on one of the major problems with the rails: they are not service conscious. We have talked today about a few successful railroads, and one of them is represented here because it is service conscious. I think the trouble in the Northeast is that the rails are not really concerned about giving service. Paul Roberts, in his paper, talked about the small role played by piggyback. That is because of the service features. When we cannot get rail cars, we go to truck. We use a little bit of piggyback and we would use more if the rails' concept of service matched our concept of service. Where it does not, we have the highway movement. Any successful transportation company is being used because it is giving the shippers service at a reasonable cost. Until that concept changes in intermodal transportation, it is just not going to work.

MR. BARNUM: Kenneth McLaughlin might want to make some observations on what the shippers have been saying about multimodal companies being a "ho-hum" issue.

MR. McLaughlin: I am intrigued that the title selected for this seminar refers to barriers to multimodal ownership. I went back to the definition of the word. A barrier is any obstruction that hinders approach or attack. Multimodal ownership is being attacked by some people and supported by other people, and we even have neutral people here.

Rodney Eyster's paper defines very clearly the barrier that faces the regulated freight forwarding industry with respect to multimodal ownership. Freight forwarders cannot own Part I, Part II, or Part III carriers (railroads, trucks, domestic water carriers), but those carriers can own a freight forwarder. Mr. Eyster explains that our present regulatory predicament is a result of the fact that freight forwarders were once considered unruly adolescents, needing protection against excessive infighting by preservation of the status quo.

I take exception here only to the statement that we were in a weak and chaotic condition—motor carriers back in those days, yes; freight forwarders, no. Of the three leading domestic freight forwarders at the time of regulation, all were healthy; two were controlled by railroads. Here was the real reason for the barrier preventing Part IV freight forwarders from controlling carriers subject to Parts I, II, and III: to protect the motor carriers—which were then all short-haul carriers and all adolescents—from the threat of indirect takeover by the railroads through freight forwarder ownership.

Ironically, the last forwarder controlled by a railroad was sold to

PIE about fifteen years ago. This forwarder, National Carloading, was later acquired by American Export as part of its entry into multimodal ownership. I do not have sufficient information to comment on whether American Export's failure was a result of the barriers under discussion or for other reasons. Today the situation is different, with one of the nation's largest motor carriers controlling two freight forwarders, yet forwarders are still restricted from direct ownership of regulated motor carriers.

Freight forwarders face barriers—more like handcuffs—in trying to be fully intermodal, which by day-to-day action they actually are. There is a definite place and a need for a common carrier that will assemble and consolidate, break bulk and distribute, both LTL [less than truckload] and volume shipments, other than through multimodal ownership, utilizing the most efficient means of transportation available under Part I, Part II, and Part III. Intermodalism without the forwarder as a catalyst does not work in the best interests of the shipper, but rather in the best interest of any dominant form of transportation, when multimodal ownership is not involved in the move. Since the freight forwarder is not dominant but is required by federal regulations to serve the shipping public as a common carrier, it can and must select the most cost- and service-efficient combination of carriers. Any other type of intermodalism, with or without barriers, is, at best, only interchange.

All we ask for is equal treatment. If a motor carrier can control a freight forwarder, then let a freight forwarder control a motor carrier. If a regulated motor carrier can have contractual arrangements with a railroad, then let the regulated forwarder have the same privilege. If a steamship company and a railroad can enter into joint rates, then don't stop the forwarder or the motor carrier from doing the same. Either raise or lower the barriers equally for all forms of regulated transportation or see dominance of one form at the expense of the other. The freight forwarders' present plight is a classic example of what happens when regulation is in one direction only.

Freight forwarders have no legislative protection as their competition has. My company, Universal Carloading and Distributing, is intermodal and has been for fifty years. Transway International, our parent company, is multimodal. Yet, at present, only our motor carrier divisions can enter into local contractual agreements. We cannot publish joint rates with our steamship companies. Again, either raise or lower the barriers for all forms of transportation on an equal basis.

MR. BARNUM: Jack Pearce, would you comment on what some of the shippers have been telling us? You have been active as an eloquent spokesman for the shipper community.

JACK PEARCE, Pearce & Brand: I would rather focus on what the shipper spokesmen have not said. Though Clifford Worth adverted to the fear that some large multimodal transportation company might become dominant, I have not heard any clear indication that these companies and others that gather freight from a great many origins and distribute it to a great many destinations would suffer any decrease in their ability to reach rural and urban origins, or rural and urban destinations, or suffer any significant decrease in their ability to handle any particular type of traffic or distribution.

Bill Smith has been saying the issue is kind of "ho-hum," meaning not much on the down side and not much visible on the up side, and I think Jim Springrose and Cliff Worth have perhaps tended to agree with that. But we do have one significant offsetting piece of evidence from today's discussion: anything that bothers Bob Dryden that much must have some possibility of effect—or perhaps not.

Harvey Romoff suggested that, in his experience in Canada, the type of rate regulation probably has more to do with the availability of intermodal service than does the corporate form. That leads me to suggest that we are dealing here with a question of combination, a question of how to put together different forms of regulation or nonregulation to achieve results. We have a situation in which very ingenious people are trying to work day to day with a given regulatory system, making a large number of ingenious and effective adjustments and reducing the scope of any possible inefficiencies which might result from those of regulations. They are finding a way to do the job at hand, whether the regulations make much sense or not.

It is difficult to imagine exactly what we could do if the ground rules were different. Cliff Worth has pointed out some possibilities in a very matter-of-fact way, basing his view of the possibilities on current needs. But no one can say now how many of those possibilities can be realized and how significant they would be. We have not been there, and we won't know until we get there.

We could say, "Let's stop worrying about it; there are higher priority items." And there are. We are obligated to spend our time and our money where the return may be greatest. But I would like to suggest that we consider that our annual per capita productivity increase in the last few decades has been—the last time I saw the numbers—less than 2 percent. A difference in that rate of a half a percentage point over time makes a huge difference in the welfare and the productivity of the system—that's a lot of progress. Perhaps most progress is not by huge jumps but by little steps, a little adjustment here and a little adjustment there.

While we address some larger regulatory issues, we should not lose sight of the possibility that some greater regulatory freedom as to rates and certificate structures might eventually produce some incremental gains per year worth having.

Third Topic: How would the formation of multimodal companies affect transportation labor?

MR. BARNUM: Can we turn now to the effect that the formation of multimodal companies might have on labor and ask Bill Mahoney to lead off. Bill was asked by the Railway Labor Executive Association to address this question on their behalf and, Bill, the floor is yours.

WILLIAM G. MAHONEY, Highsaw, Mahoney & Friedman: Most of you probably do not know me. I am a lawyer in Washington, D.C., and I have represented railroad labor organizations and airline labor organizations for about twenty-six years.

The answer to whether the formation of multimodal companies would affect transportation labor must be in the affirmative. For some individual employees and groups of employees, those effects ultimately might be beneficial. For others, both individuals and groups, jobs would be lost which could never be reestablished and employees would be transferred from place to place. For all employees, there most certainly would be a period of transition in which the railroads, the truck companies, and the water carriers would be experimenting, sometimes succeeding and sometimes failing, but always adjusting the emphasis of their operations from mode to mode, in various regions, until the optimum combinations were achieved. Whether a particular employer were to operate its company as a single entity, as a multimodal monolith, or whether it were to pit one of its modal operations against another, the adverse effects upon the individual employees would be the same. Certainly there would be a loss—to some degree, at least—in employee morale, and employee unrest would extend throughout the transportation industry, since the employees would have no idea what was going to happen next in their company.

I do not believe one can rely safely upon the Canadian experience to predict the effects on employees. In Canada, multimodal companies began with the industry itself and grew as that nation and the transportation needs of that nation grew. Transportation in the United States evolved in a totally different manner. To modify either nation's transportation system necessarily would thrust extensive hardship upon employees of that industry. For example, extensive and severe disruption and hardship would occur among employees in Canada, I am sure, if the multimodal restrictions of the United States were suddenly imposed on the Canadian transportation industry.

There would appear to be no overwhelming demand around this table, or even in this country, for the creation of multimodal transportation services on an industrywide or a nationwide scale. Almost all of us recognize that multimodal operation, with or without multimodal ownership, is not a panacea for transportation problems. Such operations carry with them certain inherent liabilities as well as risks, which may outweigh the benefits they could provide.

But if we assume for a moment the inevitability of the removal of government restrictions and the enthusiastic adoption by the industry of multimodal operations, what would most likely occur to transportation labor? Of course, any detailed or specific answer to such a question would be most speculative. But given the attitude of the immediate past administration of the Department of Transportation, which appears to be perpetuated by the present administration, one could conclude that the rail network of this nation would be reduced to three or four main lines east and west and three or four main lines north and south, and all branch lines and secondary main lines would be eliminated. The branch lines would be replaced by trucks to feed the main lines; the traffic on the secondary main lines would be combined with traffic on the main lines; and over-the-road long-haul trucking would become, for the most part, a relic of the past. Specialized containerization equipment would be introduced for pickup about the countryside and delivery to the railroad for the long-haul movement, and there would be similar equipment at the other end for delivery to the consignee. As end-to-end mergers were encouraged by the Interstate Commerce Commission, and perhaps also by the Department of Transportation, the rail haul would become longer and the truck haul shorter.

All of this would seem to injure motor carrier employees and benefit railroad employees, but that would not be the case. Employees in both modes would be seriously affected. While the over-the-road long-haul truckers would be adversely affected, and perhaps some short-haul truckers as well, over-the-road drivers would receive more work as would others involved in trucking, such as mechanics and clerical employees. Train crews on the railroads in some instances would enjoy increased work, but the crews of branch line and secondary main line trains would receive less work or none. Adverse effects would also befall the employees who maintain the tracks, the signals, and the equipment now operating on the branch and secondary main lines, because those lines would be abandoned—no question about it. These abandonments would involve thousands of miles of railroad in this country.

The motor carrier and the rail industries operate under two entirely different labor laws, and their contractual arrangements are also dissimilar. Consequently, one would expect that a multimodal company would attempt to keep the operations of its various modes as separate as possible so as not to have conflict among the employees of the different modes or their respective representatives. If one mode were to become economically or numerically dominant in a particular company, however, it would seem inevitable that, unless there was a no-raiding pact, the bargaining agents or agent of the employees of the dominant mode would seek one day to represent all the employees of the company. Should that occur, it would most certainly signal similar actions throughout the country, as both defensive and offensive measures.

Therefore, it seems to me that any statutory or regulatory move toward multimodal operations in this country must contain provisions to protect the interests of the individual employees who will be affected by it, as well as safeguards against the serious problems of representation which I just noted. Without such protections and safeguards, the probable cost of multimodal operations in the United States, in terms of employee morale and labor relations, would be much too great for the results which I believe could be realized.

I have not addressed myself to the effects on employees of multi-modal ownership between, say, rails and barges or rails and ocean-going carriers, because I felt that the greatest effects would be from multimodal ownership between rail and truck. I see little direct effect on employees of a multimodal company made up of an ocean-going carrier and a railroad. There would be more adverse effects from the combination of a barge line and a railroad because, although they would operate end-to-end, the barge line would certainly parallel another railroad line and would be in competition with it. In that event, if diversion took place, the employees of the second railroad would be adversely affected.

J. JOSEPH COTTER, administrative assistant to the general president, International Brotherhood of Teamsters, Chauffeurs, Warehousemen & Helpers of America: [11] There is far too little information concerning multimodal transportation to determine the effect on labor generally and on the members of the Teamsters' union. If multimodal transportation were conducted by a single total transportation company whose motivation and continuing purpose were to use the most efficient mode for each segment of transportation, an assessment of the impact on labor could be undertaken. The task would be difficult and involve assumptions and conjectures, but it would be possible. As Harvey Romoff points out in his paper, however, the Canadian Pacific has found that this method of operation does not work in practice. In the

---

[11] Mr. Cotter's remarks are from a paper prepared by Frank E. Fitzsimmons, general president of the International Brotherhood of Teamsters, Chauffeurs, Warehousemen & Helpers of America, who was unable to attend the seminar.

Canadian experience, each mode has been treated as an individual profit center in order to improve modal efficiency. Therefore it seems to me, at this preliminary stage in the evaluation of multimodal transportation, that careful consideration needs to be given to the information developed at this seminar on this complex and controversial subject. From my review of the papers,[12] it is apparent that theory often collides with practice and experience. Means often interfere with ends. A conclusion—even a consensus—on multimodal transportation seems unlikely in the near future. Further careful thought will have to be given to the diverse views expressed by the participants in this seminar, and I hope that the American Enterprise Institute will continue its research in this area.

The Teamsters' union has not adopted a policy regarding multimodal transportation. We have an open mind and are keenly interested. We recognize that the surface transportation industry in which we have a huge stake is not healthy. Many trucking companies, both large and small, have gone into bankruptcy in recent years. Others are on the brink of insolvency. Owner-operators are leaving the industry in substantial number because they are unable to make ends meet. Our union is dedicated to finding solutions for these unsound conditions in the motor carrier industry.

Motor carriers are not alone in being afflicted with financial problems. Many of their primary intermodal competitors, the railroads, are experiencing economic difficulties. Most of the railroads in the East have gone through bankruptcy, and their services have been restored only through the injection of billions of dollars by the federal treasury. Two major western railroads are now in bankruptcy, the Rock Island and the Milwaukee.

Despite these serious economic problems in the surface transportation industry, some government officials, including some members of the ICC, are primarily concerned that shippers, sometimes referred to as consumers, continue to enjoy cheap rates and redundant services. This attitude permits, even encourages, industrial giants, such as Sears, Roebuck, Ford Motor Company, General Motors, and General Foods, to play one mode of transportation off against another to obtain substandard rates. In the name of competition government officials encourage a multiplicity of carriers far in excess of the number required to provide good service. The rates of return of motor carriers are depressed while the rates of return of the shippers are excessive by comparison. Like their Canadian counterparts, as described by Mr. Romoff, American surface carriers are diversifying out of transportation. Railroads and motor carriers are forming holding companies to invest in

---

[12] In Part I, above.

nontransportation enterprises because the rates of return in transportation are totally inadequate.

The Teamsters' union welcomes all efforts to improve the economics of motor carrier transportation. We recognize that improvement is required now. Any idea that offers this potential will receive our thoughtful study. We are good listeners and our attitude is cooperative.

PAUL HALL, president, Seafarers International Union of North America, and president, Maritime Trades Department, AFL-CIO: [13] As a representative of sea-going labor, I appreciate the opportunity to comment on multimodal ownership in transportation. I would like to deal with the broad issues of public policy that affect the development of multimodal transportation. As a member of the maritime industry, I believe multimodal ownership is a logical evolution for the transportation network of this country. For particular companies, at particular times, it obviously has not always worked. But, in principle, it is likely to lead to greater efficiencies in our transportation system.

In my view it is essential to the national interest that marine transportation be integrated for the first time into the total transportation network of this country. This has not yet occurred because many of the people who make policy in Washington do not accept the idea that deep-sea transportation should be an American venture. As a consequence, ocean transportation has become the stepchild of the American transportation network.

Let me compare ocean transportation with the other modes in this country. If a company in North Dakota wanted to ship to the Far East 1,000 tons of some commodity, it might use any of a number of modes depending on the nature of the product and other factors. That commodity might be shipped to the West Coast by rail, in which case the 1,000 tons of cargo would have to travel entirely on an American-owned and operated railroad. In the United States, as in most other developed countries, foreign railroads are not allowed to carry American freight. If the commodity were shipped by truck, it would travel to the West Coast entirely on American-owned and operated vehicles. Here again, foreign trucking companies are not allowed to carry American cargo. If the product moved by pipeline, again it would be through a U.S.-owned and operated pipeline system. If the product moved by air, all of it would have to go on American-owned and operated aircraft.

After it reaches the West Coast, however, the entire picture changes. There is no policy in this country to require the use of Amer-

---

[13] Mr. Hall was unable to attend the conference, and the paper that he had prepared (which is given here in its entirety) was summarized at the conference by W. J. Amoss.

ican-owned and operated equipment to move products overseas. In the absence of such a national policy, U.S.-flag carriage has fallen to 5 percent of our foreign trade. I suggest that it is in the national interest to change this policy.

I think it is essential that the United States have a strong railway system. It is essential to have a strong trucking industry and highway network. We need an elaborate pipeline distribution system, just as we must have a healthy airline industry. We need all of these components if we are to maintain a strong economy and a strong national defense. But if we stop there and leave out the last link in the chain, we are doing a great disservice to the national interest. The only way to change this is to apply the same rules and the same policies to our foreign commerce that we apply to our domestic commerce. I am not suggesting that 100 percent of U.S. foreign trade be carried on U.S.-flag ships, but I do believe that the economic and defense needs of this country require substantially more than 5 percent, which is what we have now. By policy, by law, by rule, by regulation, we should be encouraging U.S. companies that operate equipment in the other transportation modes to integrate with new or existing operators of American equipment on the high seas.

From its earliest days until the 1950s, the United States was traditionally a leading maritime nation. The technical and institutional revolutions that have given multimodal ownership its great potential make it more important now than ever before that the United States become once again a leading maritime nation. Furthermore, I would suggest that, contrary to what some people claim, the cost of U.S. operations should not be the overriding factor. As a matter of national policy, we have accepted the cost of U.S. operations in other modes, and in the national interest we should do the same for ocean transportation.

We hear much about the importance of free trade and free markets, and I agree that wherever possible free trade should be encouraged and preserved. But we have to look at this realistically. We have to recognize that free-trade arguments may save us a dollar in the short run, but in some cases the long-run costs can be enormous. It is easy to succumb to the temptation to save a buck by allowing foreign countries, for example, to dump their surplus steel and surplus ships into U.S. markets. But after our industries and institutions have been destroyed, we might find reasons other than cost for keeping them alive and prosperous.

I sometimes think that in the year 2000 there are going to be only two kinds of people still employed in this country. There will be the boards of directors of a handful of multinational corporations, all of whose employees will be foreign nationals working overseas, and there will be another handful of academic economists preaching the values of free trade.

There is substantial precedent for a policy to assure the viability of a U.S. ocean-transport capability. I am not referring to the cargo preference laws of some forty-five other maritime nations in this world. I am referring to a precedent in U.S. policy whereby this country has had the good judgment to require bilateral agreements with other countries before their aircraft are permitted to land in this country. In part as a result of that policy, U.S. airlines carry a substantial portion of our airborne foreign commerce. This is as it should be. Under existing law, the same policy guidelines have been established for ocean-borne commerce. U.S. policy, according to the Merchant Marine Acts of 1936 and 1970, is that U.S.-flag ships carry a substantial share of our foreign trade—and I do not think that means 5 percent. The problem is that no one has provided the means to implement that policy. I think it is time we do. Once we establish the rules and guidelines and incentives to encourage a U.S. maritime transportation capability, we will find that, just as American ingenuity and creativity made the leading operators successful in other transportation modes, the same qualities will enable them to integrate shipping into their network and make that work, too.

Labor can support any evolution, including multimodal ownership, that will improve the transportation network of the United States, particularly ocean transportation. Since the maritime industry, among others, has become highly capital intensive, the need for participation by companies with substantial assets has grown. As long as the required changes remain legal and do not diminish competition, labor can support the growth of multimodal ownership, not only for its efficiencies, but also for its help in integrating ocean transportation into our nationwide system.

This will present an important challenge to American capitalism. The Soviet Union has already made substantial inroads into world shipping markets and will continue to expand, without regard to profit objectives as we know them, and under the guidance of a much more comprehensive social accounting system than we use in this country. It is our responsibility to make our system meet that kind of competition, especially in those areas such as marine transportation where our present shortcomings are critical. It is an opportunity for profits for U.S. companies, paying U.S. taxes, employing U.S. workers who badly need jobs. At the same time, it is a chance to add that last vital link to an integrated U.S. transportation network with important benefits to national security and the American economy. There is no excuse for the uneven treatment of different transportation modes in this country. Why not give American ingenuity a chance to prove that a comprehensive transportation system can best serve this country's needs?

MR. HILTZHEIMER: Paul Hall's paper touched upon the real problem facing the U.S.-flag ocean carrier industry, which is the absence in our country today of any coordinated, realistic policy supported by government agencies. This became apparent in certain congressional hearings and testimony by heads of various government agencies—I think there are about sixteen that have some relation to the ocean carrier industry. In their testimony it was obvious that they either did not understand the existing policy, or they misinterpreted it, or they frustrated it. As a result, the many government agencies involved with ocean carriers are challenging each other and misinterpreting the existing policy. I would be the first to admit, however, that although a good environment in which to operate is urgently needed, it is no guarantee that ocean carriers would be more profitable or successful.

In the often hostile international atmosphere today, our own government is nonsupportive of U.S. industry. Our laws actually offer an incentive to foreigners to come in and raid U.S. markets. The United States today is the only major trading nation in the world that guarantees the right of any foreigner to enter or leave its trade whenever he chooses, without any responsibility. Foreigners are attracted to the U.S. trade because it is the most lucrative trade in the world—not to belabor the point, but I couldn't resist the temptation to mention it. We have heard from representatives of labor that they, at least, are open-minded enough to support change if the end result would benefit the industry and the people they represent. They are willing to take a look at it, and that is a beginning.

MR. BARNUM: I would like to ask Bill Mahoney a question. From your remarks, I gather that you believe that one of the consequences of the opportunity to form multimodal transportation companies would be a shift of certain traffic, in some areas principally from rail to truck. But you also suggested that there would be an increase in some long-haul rail traffic as a consequence. Do you suggest that there would be a diminution of the ton-miles on rail, as distinguished from the move of some short-haul rail traffic to trucks and some long-haul truck traffic to rails? Do you come out with a plus or minus on the rail ton-miles?

MR. MAHONEY: It is difficult to say. I think, very probably, that in rail ton-miles there may be less traffic. The actual tonnage carried would probably be more, but it would be over fewer miles.

MR. BARNUM: If we assume that there would be the same number of ton-miles, albeit more tonnage over the longer hauls, would this not require the transfer of rail labor away from the shorter haul to service the more concentrated long-haul rail movements?

MR. MAHONEY: There is no question about it.

MR. BARNUM: It would be a relocation, rather than elimination, of a demand for rail labor?

MR. MAHONEY: No, there would be a relocation certainly, but there also would be a lesser demand. I don't think there is any question about that because the number of miles of track to be serviced would be cut back and there would be less need for maintenance of the signals, of the tracks, and of the roadbeds themselves. The demand for labor to maintain the equipment may or may not be affected, but there would certainly be a great move to centralize the maintenance facilities near the rail. There would probably be many fewer train crews because there would be fewer trains—larger and heavier trains, but fewer operating. As I visualize it, since the shorter-haul truck would take the place of the branch line crew, there would be fewer employees. In that sense, productivity would be much higher per employee.

MR. BARNUM: That is what I was thinking as you enumerated what some of the specific consequences might be. To be sure, the increase in total productivity would be at the cost of a number of rail labor jobs.

MR. AMOSS: May I ask a question in that regard? Isn't that the situation now, and isn't it expanding rather rapidly even without intermodal ownership? I fail to see that the fact of intermodal ownership either expands or retards the kind of concerns you have expressed. We already have branch lines that are not being maintained, and the people who would maintain them are not being employed; we have longer trains; and we are seeing a decline in the overall ton-miles in railroad operations, at least in terms of the ratio of tons that are moving. So I don't know that blame for the development of these circumstances should be placed on multimodal ownership alone. It seems to me these circumstances are here already.

MR. MAHONEY: I think we are quite a way from where we would be if we had multimodal ownership. If we were to cut back the railroads to, say, four or five east-west and north-south mainlines—which is what I see as the ultimate end of multimodal ownership—many of the lines that are profitable today would be abandoned. Branch lines that are at least marginally profitable, or that break even or lose very little, would be abandoned. The type of transportation system would be changed. When that occurred, maintenance facilities that are now on rail lines would be closed or moved and perhaps enlarged at other points to take care of this mainline flow of traffic. But it would be a different type of system.

What Mr. Amoss was referring to, I believe, is a situation in which business on branch lines is lost, say, to trucks, and the line is closed down. There may be one train three times a week or something like that, and finally the line is shut down and allowed to rust because there is no business there. It is a slow process of erosion. But many lines that are still profitably in operation would be shut down as a result of multimodal operation or ownership. We are not quite to where Mr. Amoss seems to think we may be.

MR. AMOSS: I cannot speculate on whether the lines would or would not shut down. My experience tells me that if the business is there, management will make the line work. I have seen that happen many times.

MR. MAHONEY: The latest AAR [Association of American Railroads] statistical survey points out that from 1966 to 1976 the number of railroad employees decreased 23.5 percent. The revenue ton-miles increased 7.5 percent during that same period. Would you agree that attempts to promote multimodal ownership could accelerate the process you have already perceived as taking place?

MR. AMOSS: No, because I see an acceleration in the process even without multimodal ownership, because transportation systems are being viewed more and more as a national system. The shipping community in trying to reduce costs and ultimate consumer prices—or whatever their motivation—is working more and more toward multiservice transportation, irrespective of who owns the companies. I think that has a far greater impact on the concerns of labor, in both trucking and other forms of transportation, than does the fact that ownership of a given corporation might be multimodal in nature. There may well be only four transcontinental railroads running east and west and four running north and south because, at least in my view, there are far more corporate railroad entities in the United States than the commerce can support. The whole system raises very grave issues that concern many people and that are irrespective of who owns what corporation.

MR. MAHONEY: As I said when I started, the thrust of the transportation policy of the last administration has been to cut down the number of rail lines to four or five east and west and four or five north and south. Whatever the number, there would be fewer mainlines with no branches, and the mainlines would be fed by trucks. I say that change would come more quickly and certainly would be accelerated if one company owned, say, one of those four east-west lines plus a number of truck lines to feed it.

MR. SHAY: I would like to ask a question of Joseph Cotter, and I don't mean it to be a loaded one. I realize that 60 percent of the revenue dollar of the motor carrier goes for labor costs and fringe benefits, and that the total number of owner-operators—a large segment of our trucking industry, especially in the area of exempt commodities—is diminishing. On top of these problems are the economic difficulties of existing for-hire carriers. Naturally and consequently, I would assume that the number of active or employed teamsters is diminishing.

Has the Teamsters' union given any thought to dealing with the individual situations? All trucks are not alike. They are made out of the same material and have the same kind of tires, but that is about the only resemblance among the various operations. Do you think there is any way to stem this erosion of employment of teamsters? The tonnage is increasing so something is happening. Perhaps we have a one package, one truck deal, like the phenomenon of one passenger, one car that presented a great dilemma for mass passenger transportation. Is any thought being given to dealing with the various segments separately or to tailoring negotiations to fit a particular one, instead of handling the problem at the national level?

MR. COTTER: No, not at this time. We are concerned about the motor carrier industry and about the financial condition of some of the companies in the industry. We will probably be confronted by an additional problem April 1 when, as a result of our present National Master Freight Agreement, which includes a cost-of-living clause along with a fifty cent an hour wage increase, the motor carrier operators will be faced with an eighty-eight cent an hour increase. This figure could go up or down a penny, depending on the final cost-of-living adjustment.

We are in the process of completing a detailed survey, which we hope will give us an idea of the number of over-the-road drivers and owner-operators in the car-haul industry, in the tank-haul industry, as well as in the dry freight field. William Mahoney raised some very serious problems concerning rails and over-the-road operations. We most certainly want to get involved and improve the industry wherever possible.

MR. BARNUM: Mr. Cotter, an earlier speaker made reference to the provision in some of the Teamster agreements—I believe it is in the National Master Freight Agreement—that limits a motor carrier's use of piggyback service, unless he does not have enough over-the-road drivers. This was described as an inhibition on intermodal transportation, without regard to the multimodal companies. As long as it was there, the speaker suggested, a railroad or, for that matter, a motor carrier would not be inclined to invest in equipment that could be used only on those occasions when the National Master Freight Agreement permits use of the piggyback service.

This has been described elsewhere as a barrier to multimodal ownership that is as economically effective as some of the statutes. Do you see any other way to protect the teamsters and yet give the motor carriers or the multimodal companies greater flexibility to move the freight by whatever method proves to be the most efficient? Do you see any way other than economic or contractual constraint on the motor carrier?

MR. COTTER: I have not heard of piggyback's being a problem in the last ten years. It was a problem when piggyback started to come in and take the long hauls. We do not have a problem with piggyback now.

MR. PEARCE: Part of what Bill Mahoney was saying seemed to me to express a certain amount of fear of the dislocating effects on labor of a shift in traffic with multimodal operation. If I may hypothesize, perhaps that apprehension comes from the importance of the job to the individual laborer. The job is the breadbasket; it determines or is related to where and how the worker lives. But the railroad industry obviously has severe financial problems in portions of it and severe limitations on all of it. To relate this to the regulatory system, we have all of these regulations because, at least once, the railroads were tremendously important to the country and to the shippers. It would be rather odd if the railroads were so important to us that we could not afford to allow them to be more successful.

MR. MAHONEY: The point I was trying to make was that the dislocation of employees happens all the time. It happened during the merger movement of the railroads and continues today. And if we were to have multimodal operations that would dislocate employees, then the interest of the employee should be protected. That was the thrust of the whole statement.

Address to the Conference

Brock Adams

I am particularly interested in your topic today. It is one of the reasons I was glad to accept when I was asked to come over and spend a few minutes with you. I have two or three ideas that I want to throw out to this group of well-known and experienced people in the transportation field before I float them in the public area. I hope also to give you a little food for thought during the course of the afternoon while you are discussing intermodalism. I am not even sure I like the word "intermodalism." I have some real questions about that. I am also a little frightened, as I look around the room, because I see a lot of old friends who are heavyweights in the transportation business. I could be in a great deal of trouble, in trying to be very light, because you may be looking toward what we might be doing and how we might be doing it.

I am constantly reminded that in the transportation field there are no final solutions. I no longer talk about a light at the end of the tunnel because the first time I tried that somebody said to me, "In transportation, that means the Lincoln Tunnel and the light at the end of that tunnel is New York City." So I do not come to you with that kind of a message. I do come to you with a message about the energy problem that we must all repeat over and over again. It is real. It will not go away. The President of the United States is involved, I am involved, and all of you here are deeply involved in it. Whatever you want to call the present energy situation—a crisis, a shortage, an allocation adjustment, whatever it is—we have a very big problem and one that must be addressed.

Whether that problem is going to be solved through the price mechanism, with fuel costs becoming a major factor, or by conversion from one kind of fuel to another, energy today is bedrock basic to transportation discussions and fundamental to intermodalism. I cannot get the American people to buy it now, but I am trying. I think it is the responsibility of the secretary of transportation because, otherwise, along about 1984 or 1985 or 1987 people are going to ask, "Why didn't you tell us we were going to have some real problems with a petroleum-based economy moving through the 1980s?"

The problem, as we all know, is that we do not control the source of supply for the petroleum we require today. We are now over 50 percent dependent on foreign supplies. Nobody at this point has yet figured a way to go back to using the steam locomotive or to electrify the system. We are very much bound into petroleum-based motor transportation, air transportation, rail transportation and, yes, even water transportation. In other words, transportation is the largest single user of a petroleum resource that is nonconvertible. We can convert utilities. We can convert certain stationary sources. But we are not capable of running our vehicles with either nuclear power or coal power or any other kind of power—and I have listened to proposals for gasohol and all the others—between now and the year 1990.

We have to address this issue because, in a democratic society, logic precedes necessity, which is then followed by action. We are at the logic stage right now, but the fact that we are logical about it does not necessarily mean we move the American people. As long as gasoline flows freely at the pump, the problem seems far off. But if we get to the necessity stage, it is going to be like a tidal wave if we have not made the appropriate decisions. When that tidal wave hits, everybody is going to have to swim like mad to maintain a private enterprise economy in a crunch.

Why do I bring this up in a discussion on intermodalism? Because I am convinced from over two decades of working with transportation people that shippers are concerned about just three things: cost, reliability, and safety. They want to know how much it is going to cost, how long it is going to take to get there, and whether it is going to get there in the same condition in which it was sent. Those of us in transportation systems may care, but shippers do not care whether the freight is put on a barge, a railroad car, a truck, a horse, or carried on someone's back. They just want to know how long, how much, and will it get there. We have seen a tremendous shift from the days of the water monopoly to the time of the rail monopoly to the present system where there really is no monopoly except in spot situations.

I am concerned from the standpoint of fuel consumption that, for example, we in transportation cannot deliver fresh produce from California to New York, from Florida to New York, or elsewhere throughout this country, other than by putting it aboard a refrigerated truck, filling that truck with petroleum, and running it the length of the United States. When the ultimate energy crunch in petroleum occurs, we had better be ready with an alternative to that system.

How do we get change? How do we get people to focus on the problem? Right now the truck is competitive from California to New York because the shipper, looking at the three factors of cost, reliability, and safety, figures that the extra cost is worth the price. And that is the market.

Remember what happened with the apple harvest during the fuel embargo. Senator Magnuson and I both talked with many people, some of you in this room today, who had been shipping by truck for a long time. Then suddenly the fuel was gone, and all those apples were sitting out there, and there was no way they were going to get moved. The shippers wanted the railroad cars, and the railroad companies said, "All right. We are ready to come back, but we are not going to re-ice and reconfigure our fleets and provide the cars unless you guarantee to stay with us." But when the oil embargo went away so did the railroad cars, and we were back where we started. Because this situation can repeat itself, we are trying to say that transportation policy must revive alternatives in the marketplace for the movement of goods and the movement of people.

The second point I want to make is the need to make better use of existing rights-of-way. This is a difficult position for a secretary of transportation to take. Secretaries of transportation are known as great constructors of public works and monuments, and that is what our constituency wants. If we lose that constituency, we rapidly become unsuccessful and unpopular. But I believe that we must make better use of our existing rights-of-way. We hear it from governors, from people in the private sector, from local government officials, and from people on Capitol Hill: "Don't lay a big new system on us. We can't afford it."

We do not know how we are going to repair what we have. How do we make sure the lock and dam system continues to function? Some of those facilities are fifty years old. How do the railroads, some of which have let their right-of-way go down, manage to stay functional so that the essential links are still there? We have to complete the interstate highway program, close the gaps, and then see that the thing stays in place and does not completely deteriorate. Otherwise, we will have spent billions of dollars for a system that is nonusable. We have to shift over to make better use of the systems we have because we have only a limited amount of money. To fund the programs that people have in mind for transportation or to build gigantic new systems would require more money than could possibly be collected. In other words, we must take whatever resources are available and try to use them in the best place, because there is no way we can meet all the demands.

To give some examples, on Capitol Hill we have a program that has dedicated $2 billion to bridges alone, but the cost estimates for the program run anywhere from $30 to 40 billion. There probably are $30 to 40 billion worth of bridges in this country that need to be fixed or replaced, but we don't have the money to fix $30 to 40 billion worth of bridges.

Maintenance costs are another item. The states cannot afford to

123

maintain the interstate highways. The original plan was "We build it, you fix it," but it is not working that way. The states are saying they cannot even maintain their primary roads. That concerns me. But we must understand that there is a finite amount of money, and most of that money must go into making the systems we have work better.

I am having a real problem in the Midwest keeping the railroads going. Ensuring that the tracks are there and that service is maintained is going to cost a great deal of money. And I am not anxious to impose a Northeast-type solution on the Midwest. I believe we can develop a system in the Midwest that will work in the private sector.

Now, I want to talk to you a bit about the intermodal problem of regulation and how it might be approached. I think that removing the barriers to intermodal transportation systems, be they regulatory or otherwise, is absolutely necessary if we are going to put money into the system and make the system work better.

The original barrier to trucks' owning railroads, railroads' owning trucks, railroads' owning ship lines, and vice versa came—and I hate even to mention the name—in the Panama Canal Act of 1912. The provision was put in almost as an aside to prevent a monopoly and to protect the trade through the Panama Canal. The treaty negotiators did not want the railroads to buy up all the intercoastal shipping lines. At that time we had a much different transportation mix than we have now, when less than 40 percent of the traffic of the United States is carried by rail. Moreover, the prohibition which was written in was not absolute but was simply an instruction to the regulatory agencies that there should not be intermodal ownership. On that instruction was built an entire body of law—a patchwork of a piece of statutory language here and a regulatory ruling there—that said never the twain shall meet. In other words, a truck line cannot own a railroad, nor can a railroad own a truck line, a ship line, and so on. We grandfathered some of those provisions so that the prohibition has not been absolute, but the whole thrust of years of regulation through the ICC was to prohibit intermodal ownership.

I would like to suggest that the provision be changed, and I throw it out to all of you because I hope you will work on it this afternoon. We ought to see whether we can have intermodal ownership of systems—by that I mean whether a truck line should be allowed to own a railroad as well as a railroad allowed to own a truck line and a barge line.

This of course presents some real problems, for example, the problem of transportation monopolies. If somebody in a small town is running a truck line, no matter how much talk there is about free entry, that local operator is no more going to be able to compete against a major transportation conglomerate that owns trucks and rails and barges than the Milwaukee was able to compete against the Burlington Northern—though everybody said it would compete. In other words, we do not create situations just by saying they are going to happen.

I hope you will discuss the conglomerates now in the transportation business. I would much rather see them diversify into other transportation activities than into other kinds of business. It is very hard to rally support for the transportation industry when it says it is in trouble, if conglomerates are placing their funds in other kinds of businesses. They claim it is legitimate for them to do that because they are not able to make any money in their own industry, and they are supporting transportation with what they are doing outside.

A number of large railroad companies now have trucking subsidiaries under the grandfather clause. Why not consider the possibility of some cross-country truckers getting into the railroad business? I can see a number of railroad presidents turning rather ashen at that thought. But I suggest you ought to think about it a bit because trucking is no longer a mom-and-pop business in a small town running a few trucks back and forth. There are some major financial interests there.

I am always afraid that the management of a particular conglomerate will decide that it is really running a railroad and will use trucks wherever it can but will not be too concerned about them. I do not want to create any red team, green team type of operation, but an appropriate point to start the discussion is the best possible use of fuel and equipment and rights-of-way, and that means the ability to shift the modes as needed. Running railroad cars on sidings in and out of major cities is breaking certain railroad companies. Long-distance truck hauls often are very fuel inefficient and not efficient in carrying traffic. I would like to see a system where distribution and pickup can combine with long haul for the best use of both, and I would like to know what you come up with in your discussions here today to achieve this.

We face a problem in the Northeast, for example, of how to pick up from a number of sources and make that system viable. A terminal railroad system is extremely difficult to run, but, on the other hand, throwing trucks out on the road for long distances is also hard. So you ought to think about that a bit and talk to me about how they might go together. In my opinion, there is little doubt that distribution and collection and relatively short-haul traffic is most efficiently done with a motor vehicle, and that long-haul traffic is best done by rail, particularly if there is control of trackage over a distance. As I said earlier, the shipper does not care which one carries the freight as long as the system works. But the biggest problem is at linkage points, when trying to shift from one mode to another or even from one carrier to another within the same mode.

I think the industry has matured. We are living in the age of large financial conglomerates that do some interesting and different things. I do not mind if the shipper wants to own the whole thing because I face the problem, together with a lot of other people in this room, of how to make a system work. The government is trying to keep rail service going and to see that the trucking people prosper, and the thrust of government is toward service throughout the country. We are not properly tapping our potential capital resources for developing that system. But I am hopeful that some of you will have suggestions for us as to how we can best approach the problem, and that is my message for today.

Discussion

MR. SHAY: I am Howard Shay from New York, Mr. Secretary, and I heard you say that there were no more mom-and-pop operations in this business. I would like you to have something to think about this afternoon. There are 10,000 of us waiting in catchment or commercial zones and the railhead areas—whatever you want to call terminal areas—10,000 of us waiting to go into intermodalism with any other mode, and to establish rules and joint rates. We are ready to perform this intermodalism service with 10,000 very efficiently run mom-and-pop operations.

SECRETARY ADAMS: I thank you. I receive your message. I have heard it before—and, Pop, I want to tell you that I am trying to determine a way that you can get a piece of the action.

MR. HILTZHEIMER: Mr. Secretary, would it be correct to say that you have broadened your view on multimodal ownership because of the economies that logically can be reached and the less fuel that will be needed in the future to move the same tonnage as now?

SECRETARY ADAMS: Have I arrived at my position because of the fuel economies and the economies of movement? The answer is yes. Certain systems in the United States are beginning to economize on their fuel consumption, and I want to see it happen elsewhere. We have to have a better collection system, one that goes onto the long-haul system, rather than have both systems operating with a built-in inefficiency. That is what I am trying to say and what I want people to think about.

In some operations, for example, where coal is picked up at the mine and delivered to the utility, don't worry about what I said. Forget it and just keep hauling coal back and forth. What I am concerned about is the pickup of general commodities and the things that cannot use a regular bulk operation. In the movement of various agricultural

126

products the situation is either a feast or a famine. In the Midwest, we need a transport capacity built for harvest. At harvest time there are never enough cars, never enough people, and everybody is mad. But about 90 percent of the time nothing is happening, and there is a problem of underutilization of the system. The same thing applies to the truck operators that follow the harvest throughout the country. They are now becoming angry because, as fuel costs go up, they cannot control their fuel dumps. They get left wherever they happen to be. In addition, their operation becomes inefficient unless they are very sophisticated, and many are not. It is hard to be at the right place at the right time, and they often end up returning with an empty truck.

The shipper faces the converse of this situation. At a given time everybody is picking up a particular product and moving it. If another harvest comes in a little early or a little late, the shipper has to pay whatever is necessary to get it out of there. We have to try to smooth that out, and I think that is a challenge for the private sector. The government cannot say, "Tomorrow we're going to move 40,000 trucks to Florida because we're going to harvest oranges, but then we're going to move 25,000 up for peaches in Georgia," and so on. There is enormous political pressure in the United States now to help the independent owner-operator.

I keep saying that before people start handing out their patented remedy they had better talk to the carrier. They will find he is not for deregulation. He wants one of three things: he wants a rate card, which is basically a type of monopoly to ensure a certain price; or he wants to be a labor union so that he can bargain; or he wants to be a regulated carrier without the burdens of regulation. When we get out of the world of theory and down to the matter of delivery, that is what carriers will say and that is what I am trying to get everybody here to focus on. How do we solve that problem?

I do not want to see trucks running around empty in the United States, but I also feel that we cannot automatically solve the problem by deregulating everything. Then those who are providing service in the nonharvest periods would drop their service, and it would be catch as catch can. I think that we have to address that. The market will address it, but in the transportation business the market is often just far enough behind our operation so that we are dead before it gets there. That is what the farmers worry about, and that is what they complain about. Thank you all very much for listening to me.

Conference Discussion: Second Session

First Topic: Would the formation of multimodal companies affect carriers' ability to obtain financing?

MR. BARNUM: David Munro of John Hancock is a long-time investor, happy or otherwise, in transportation investments. I have asked him to lead the discussion of this topic.

DAVID M. MUNRO, second vice president, John Hancock Mutual Life Insurance Company: Hancock has about $500 million in transportation investments, and I have been involved with them for seventeen years in this area, going back to Mahaffie Act extensions and actual reorganizations and new loans. When I was asked to discuss this, I ended up taking a rather simple approach from the viewpoint of a long-term lender. The question was whether multimodal transportation companies would be better able to raise capital than would companies that are essentially limited to one mode of transportation.

Obviously there are no clear-cut answers. To me, it really depends on how logical the combination is and what form it takes. As a provider of capital, my basic objectives are a fair rate of return and assured safety of principal. If the anticipated return from a particular investment is inadequate to compensate for the risk of losing principal, then that investment will not be made, at least from the private sector.

Many common carriers have problems in raising capital today, and these problems are going to continue unless steps are taken to improve a carrier's return on investment. The two industries where I see the greatest problem are the railroads and the airlines. To the best of my knowledge, the trucking industry and barge lines have not had great problems raising money for equipment. The money has always been there, whether it be Title XI or bank financing.

Many companies in both the railroad and airline industries have already diversified outside of transportation, with mixed results. I would like to comment briefly on how diversification affects existing lenders.

When diversification takes place through a holding company, the

129

existing debt holders are segregated and do not have the benefit of the cash generated by the other entities. There is also the additional risk that management time, expertise, and cash could be drained from present operations to the detriment of current lenders. I do not see any easy way for lenders to protect themselves in this area, other than to rely upon the capability of the management and its ability to diversify soundly. An ill-conceived diversification program can and has put companies into bankruptcy, but this situation is not unique to transportation companies, and it seems to me unfair to hang that particular albatross around the neck of the transportation industry alone. Where diversification is achieved directly or through subsidiaries, present lenders will benefit from any excess cash.

Now to the question of whether the formation of multimodal companies would affect their ability to raise capital: There are three ways in which intermodal companies can be created—by direct expansion, by acquisition, and through merger. I would like to outline how a long-term lender would analyze companies interested in diversifying their transportation services. The analysis is common to all three. The restrictions are a little different.

First, we would review the purpose of the loan, that is, the equipment, terminal facilities, leveraged buy-out, or whatever. We would want to be convinced that the payback would be adequate to service the debt. We would study the projected cash flow, the assumptions underlying those projections, and the adequacy of the security, if secured.

Depending on the form of borrowing, we would analyze the existing company. We would look at the carrier's historical operating record, its operating leverage, ability to cover fixed charges, balance sheet leverage, cash flow, and corporate structure. If the expansion were to be accomplished through merger or acquisition, our task would be a little easier. We would also evaluate the historical record of the company to be acquired.

The acquiring corporation can utilize three common borrowing techniques. It can borrow direct, which enables the earnings generated by the diversification program to be available to existing and future creditors and to the stockholders. It can form a subsidiary which, possibly, could borrow on its own. It could form a holding company with operating units which could borrow independently. The last two methods are advantageous to the stockholders of the parent company but would pose some problems for the lenders. These problems can be minimized. If the loan is to be made to a subsidiary, the parent company may guarantee the new debt, or the lending institution may, and probably will, restrict the upstreaming of cash by limiting investments, advances, dividends, and so on. If the loan is to the parent company, the opposite is true. The new lenders want to ensure that there are no restrictions on cash flowing up to the parent, and future borrowing by the subsidiary would be restricted.

In summary, I think a multimodal transportation company that is properly capitalized and that has a good operating record and a sound, well-conceived plan of diversification will probably serve the public interest well and improve its rate of return, and adequate capital will be available.

MR. BARNUM: I have asked Richard Fishbein to comment on this issue from the point of view of the investment banking community.

RICHARD FISHBEIN, managing director, Lehman Brothers Kuhn Loeb Incorporated: [14] The formation of multimodal companies is likely to have a favorable effect on carriers' ability to obtain financing. In fact, this, in the long run, may be a principal reason for the formation of multimodal companies. The ability of an enterprise to obtain financing depends principally on its capacity to generate net income and cash flow in the long run. It is from net income and cash flow that lenders are repaid and stockholders are paid dividends and realize capital appreciation.

In the transportation industry, there are two other important factors. First, because much of the transportation industry's capital investment is in equipment, such as aircraft, ships, locomotives, and railroad cars that can be easily removed and used by other carriers, it is possible to finance such equipment on a secured basis through leasing and equipment trust certificates where the collateral value of the equipment is more important than the creditworthiness of the owner of the equipment. In recent years a substantial portion of new aircraft and railroad equipment has been financed in this way. Second, certain federal laws and regulations facilitate carrier financing by reducing the credit risk to the investor. Section 77 of the Federal Bankruptcy Act gives owners of railroad equipment trust certificates special status in a bankruptcy, and Title XI of the Merchant Marine Act of 1936 provides U.S. government guarantees for financing up to 87.5 percent of the cost of vessels built in the United States.

The formation of multimodal companies would not significantly affect the financing of transportation equipment on a secured basis or financing under federal laws and regulations which reduce the credit risk to the investor. It would, however, other things being equal, increase the capacity of transportation enterprises to generate net income

---

[14] Between the time of the conference and the printing of the proceedings Mr. Fishbein joined Bear, Stearns & Co. as vice president of the corporate finance department.

and cash flow in the long run and thereby increase the capacity of carriers to obtain financing.

From an investor's perspective, the various modes of transportation have different economic characteristics that affect their creditworthiness. Railroads, airlines, and ocean shipping operations tend to be capital intensive, cyclical, and characterized by a relatively high level of fixed costs. Petroleum and natural gas pipelines tend to be capital intensive and characterized by a relatively high level of fixed costs, but in recent years they have not been cyclical. Because of their capital intensiveness, these modes of transportation tend to be dominated by relatively large corporate enterprises. On the other hand, motor carriers and surface and airfreight forwarders tend to be less capital intensive, to be less cyclical, and to have a higher level of variable costs. Inland waterway operators tend to be less capital intensive and have a relatively high level of variable costs, but have been cyclical in recent years. All modes of transportation, with the exception of pipelines, are labor intensive, and all modes are subject to government regulation of tariffs and rates of return.

The combination of capital intensiveness, relatively high fixed costs, and cyclicality causes net income and cash flow to fluctuate widely in the railroad, airline, and ocean shipping industries, thus impairing their creditworthiness and ability to raise capital. At the same time, these are the modes of transportation that because of their capital intensiveness have the greatest financing needs. Moreover, the advent of a new generation of wide-body jets in the early 1980s and the increased traffic growth anticipated for the railroads as a result of their comparative energy efficiency pose additional capital requirements for airlines and railroads in the years ahead.

Insofar as multimodal companies combined capital-intensive, high fixed cost, cyclical modes with less capital-intensive, less cyclical, more variable cost modes, the formation of such companies would result, other things being equal, in stronger financial enterprises. Simply put, the combination of a railroad and a motor carrier would, other things being equal, result in an enterprise with greater stability of net income and greater generation of cash flow in the long run. Such an enterprise might well have greater capacity to finance in total and at lower cost than either enterprise independently.

This leads to a key point: The removal of barriers to the formation of multimodal companies would, in the long run, likely result in the formation of multimodal companies for financial as well as operating reasons. This would come about as capital-intensive, high fixed cost, cyclical transportation enterprises, which tend to be relatively large corporations with substantial financing needs, enter or—more likely—merge with companies in less capital-intensive, less cyclical, more variable cost modes.

The first important merger in U.S. history was the combination in 1853 of a group of New York State railroads to form the New York Central System. Since that time, business combinations have played an important role in the growth of large corporations and the structuring of the U.S. economy. Until World War II most business combinations were either horizontal, in that they combined two or more enterprises in the same stage of the production process, such as the combination of two railroads, or vertical, in that they combined two or more enterprises in successive stages of the production process, such as the combination of a steel mill and a coal mine. The principal purposes of these mergers were to increase market share or to realize operating economies or both. In recent years, conglomerate mergers, which combine two or more enterprises not otherwise related, have become important. The principal objective of conglomerate mergers is to obtain the financial advantages of diversification and size. Larger and more diversified enterprises can raise more capital at lower cost and are in a better position to weather the uncertainties of a free enterprise economy.

In the transportation industry, airlines, railroads, and shipping companies have, in recent years, pursued the advantages of diversification and size by combining with, acquiring, and in some cases starting up noncarrier activities. The removal of barriers to the formation of multimodal companies would permit the advantages of diversification and size to be obtained within the transportation industry. This could be appealing to management because of its familiarity and experience with transportation. It would, in most cases, lead to financially stronger enterprises irrespective of any operating economies of multimodal operation.

The formation of multimodal companies is something that Secretary Adams said he would favor. This is something, in my judgment, that would happen. A company like TWA, for example, which has announced a program to diversify out of the airline industry, might very well look to barge line operation or the motor carrier business rather than to nontransportation enterprises.

From a purely financial point of view, if this were to come about, it could create financially strong enterprises and, in that sense, would serve the public. It might, however, raise a different kind of issue that we, as a society, have not really faced up to. That is the question of aggregate concentration. What percentage of our productive assets do we want to be controlled by the 500 or 1,000 largest corporations in the United States? But that is a topic for another seminar.

MR. BARNUM: Our third representative from the financial community is Anthony Low-Beer of L. F. Rothschild, Unterberg, Towbin.

ANTHONY B. LOW-BEER, vice president, L. F. Rothschild, Unterberg,

Towbin: Happily or unhappily, I am a railroad analyst and therefore associated with that industry. I point this out because I would like you to know what my background is before you all start throwing tomatoes at me.

Basically I do not look at the whole problem in terms of the financeability of multimodal companies. I think financing would depend on their results, and that has already been covered. The real question that we have to face, I feel, is a different one: How do we, as a country or government, feel about market shares of transportation? Do we want to subsidize one mode and not another, and how do we feel about intermodal companies?

First I would like to comment on what would happen if multimodal companies were to be allowed. I defy anybody to claim realistically that truck and barge lines would go out and bid for railroads. One participant this morning wished his competitor would go out and buy a railroad, and that, I think, reflects the sentiment quite well. Railroads are generally bigger than the other modes: the three largest railroads have revenues of $6 billion combined and net investment in plant of $7 billion. My statistical assistant tells me that the three largest truckers have revenues aggregating just under $3 billion, but net investment approximately a tenth of that of the railroads. The three largest barge companies are much smaller than the three largest truckers.

This brings us to two additional points. First, it is very difficult for a little fish to eat a big fish, even if it wants to. Therefore, the railroad will be the surviving company. Second, railroads are likely to be more serious about acquiring truck and barge lines because trucks and barges are far more profitable than railroads. Earnings based on return on net plant (that is, excluding depreciation) were just under 12 percent in 1976 for trucks, over 20 percent for barges, and just 1.6 percent for railroads. In terms of stockholders' equity, the numbers are 13.6 percent for trucks, 17.2 percent for barges, and 1.8 percent for railroads.

Under these conditions, then, if I were a stockholder of a trucking company or a barge company and I discovered that they were interested in buying a railroad, I would suggest that the management be fired. The most profitable railroads, according to rate of return, were the Southern Railway and the Norfolk & Western, and they both earn about 7.5 percent on plant and 12 percent on equity, both of which are less than the averages of the truck and the barge industries. Railroad management, however, would love to buy into a higher return industry. Thus, the truck and barge companies' managements are fearful of being swallowed up. It is obvious that the railroads are generally going to be in favor of getting into these high profit opportunities, while some of the other companies will be more fearful.

This has to be looked at from a social standpoint, though, and this is where it gets tricky. From a social standpoint, one has to ask whether it is advantageous to allow railroads to buy into the truck and barge business. Railroads say yes, that they can give better multimodal service, that it works well in Canada, and so forth. On the other hand, the truck and the barge managements are afraid of these colossal companies and believe that being under railroad ownership would result in disinvestment in their mode.

The main point to consider is the poor profit performance of the railroads and the relatively excellent profit performance of the trucks and barges. One must not forget that the railroads are the sick part of our transportation system. If the railroads were to be nationalized, it would not be beneficial to anybody. The question then becomes whether the railroad industry as a whole would be helped if its constituent companies were allowed to operate truck and barge lines. The distinction is between the railroad system as a whole and the railroad companies and their stockholders.

There are several explanations for the low rate of return of the railroad industry: labor productivity, branch lines, problems in rail management, misunderstandings in pricing and costing, and problems of government and litigation, an example of which is the coal rate case. Basically, though, one believes either that the low rate of return in the railroad industry is due to management problems, or that it is due to subsidies of other modes of transportation. If it is assumed that railroad managements are worse than trucking and barge managements, it follows that if railroads were allowed to acquire other companies they would mess up other industries. We certainly do not want that to happen, but I do not think that that is the real problem.

My view, basically, is that the trucks and the barges do not pay for their full share of right-of-way costs. The railroads do, however, and this has distorted the rate-of-return characteristics. A portion of the rate of return on the highways and the barge lines is paid by the public. For example, large trucks are requiring tougher engineering standards. We have a preliminary combined federal and state highway budget of $30.6 billion for 1978, which, I understand, includes an "appropriation" of $4.6 billion by the various levels of government to manage it. I also understand from the *Wall Street Journal* that about $50 to 70 billion is needed for deferred maintenance of the highways, a figure even greater than that apparently required for railroad maintenance, which seems surprising. The point is that the highway system is expensive. It is not being paid for entirely by the trucker. One of the reasons the railroads have such a low rate of return, I believe, is that they put 15 percent of their revenues into maintenance of way. Truck companies do not pay anything approaching 15 percent of their revenues for highway use taxes.

In the case of barges, the right-of-way costs are not paid at all, since they pay no user charges. Although this may be in the process of being changed, to date, as far as I know, it has not been.[15] Thus, one reason the railroads are unprofitable is that their competition is indirectly subsidized.

If railroads were allowed to buy truck lines and barge lines, resources would be shifted from a nonsubsidized mode to a subsidized mode because, as we in the financial community know, investment is generally made where the rate of return is highest. Since the rates of return are higher in barges and trucking than they are in railroads, if the railroads bought into these enterprises, more often than not the railroad system as a whole would suffer, and investment in trucks and barges would increase.

The weak point in the transportation system is that the low return in the railroad industry is leading to disinvestment in railroads and to deferred maintenance. What can one do about it? My answer is to alleviate the problems that caused this in the first place, namely, the subsidies on competitors' rights-of-way. Once that is done, intermodalism might make sense, but returns in railroading might be such that I am not sure whether the railroads would want it anymore.

MR. BARNUM: I first knew John Terry in his incarnation as the financial vice president of USRA [United States Railway Association]—father or godfather of Conrail—and he is an acknowledged expert in the financial area. John, I wonder if you have any observations on the comments that have been made by our panelists from the financial community.

JOHN J. TERRY, group vice president, Land Transportation, IU International Management Corporation: Because so many people do not understand the subsidy aspects of the various modes, I would like to say that the alleged subsidy that the heavy trucks received according to the 1969 highway study was, I believe, $385 million a year. It was calculated in a way that was prejudicial to the heavy trucks, because it charged them with all the incremental highway capacity.

The heavy trucks in this case are both private—General Mills' trucks, for example—and common carrier trucks; and there are more private trucks than there are common carrier trucks. When we talk about the profit of the motor carrier industry, we are talking about only the for-hire segment. It must be remembered that light trucks overpay their share into the highway fund; thus for-hire carriers should get a

---

[15] P.L. 95-502, enacted on October 13, 1978, and signed by President Carter on October 21, 1978, imposes a four cent per gallon excise tax on fuel used by barges in FY1981, increasing gradually to ten cents per gallon in FY1986.

credit for the light trucks, and I have as many pickup trucks as I do highway, intercity trucks.

A few years back I used to pay about eleven cents per gallon for diesel fuel and about eleven cents per gallon for highway tax, twenty-two cents in total. We are now paying about forty cents for the diesel fuel and the tax is about thirteen cents. In spite of that cost we have continued to gain market share from the railroads. If the highway tax had been five or six cents a gallon instead of four—I don't care how much so long as it was a fair allocation of highway costs—the increase would have gone toward operating expenses. We would have adjusted rates for it, and we would have had the same revenues and the same profits we have today.

You also have to understand that there are material subsidies to the rail industry. The billions of dollars that are being invested by the federal government in Conrail benefit the other railroads in the country because they go toward operating expenses which support the rates that the rail industry charges. Then too, the federal government has picked up, I believe, about an $8 billion deficiency in the Railroad Retirement Fund. We pay $60 per week, per man, for our health, welfare, and pension plan, and I would love to have the federal government pick up $30 of that—$20, anything—as they do for the Railroad Retirement Fund.

We have major problems in the rail industry, but I would not want people to believe that those problems were caused by the subsidies. There are things the rails should be relieved of—the real estate tax on their right-of-way is a nice simple example. They have to pay real estate tax on their right-of-way; the truckers pay for their right-of-way in fuel taxes but they do not pay real estate taxes. Maybe there is a way to resolve this simple difference. But believe me, we are not going to find the answer in this subsidy issue.

MR. LOW-BEER: Can I answer a couple of these tomatoes very quickly? I think this whole question of the highways has to be restudied. If there is $50 to 70 billion worth of deferred maintenance needed, I think it has to be determined what wear and what construction costs are caused by what. I agree with you that the pickup trucks and light trucks are not responsible; the problem is the heavy trucks.

I also think that you are right about common carrier trucks. You could get your rates. Probably the person who would be hurt most by removing subsidies is the owner-operator, and it has been politically difficult because the owner-operator would fight it. You would not care if you paid a user charge—you're right; you'd get it right back—but the owner-operator could not get it back. So the real problem here may be the owner-operator.

MR. TERRY: Typically, the owner-operators get a percentage of revenue, and to the extent that revenue is increased, their compensation goes up. So if you get rate increases to cover all added costs, the operators tend to benefit from the same increase.

I have been asked about the financial side of the multimodal companies, but I do not see it as very important. The motor carriers are having no trouble raising capital these days, except for the very small ones that are trying to raise equity capital. There is a problem in all the equity markets, and there is a big entry cost into trucking because of the purchase of the rights, which has to be done, essentially, with equity capital. Certainly, rail companies have some money that would make it possible to purchase operating rights.

So I do not see much of a problem on the financing side. Probably ten years ago—maybe fourteen now—it was much more difficult for motor carriers to raise money. In those days motor carriers had to borrow almost entirely from banks; there were not many long-term lenders. The insurance lenders have stepped in recently and are very interested in financing us, other than on a terminal basis. The banks have always been there, but formerly it was the lesser banks and rates were high. Today all the lenders are happy to lend to motor carriers. They are not very anxious to lend to rails except on the equipment securities, but I do not see much of a financing problem.

MR. FISHBEIN: I think we are all saying in different ways that, in and of itself, the formation of multimodal companies probably would not affect carriers' ability to finance. Insofar as multimodalism led to more diversified and larger companies, however, I may favor it in the long run. On the other hand, if those diversified and larger companies are not well managed, weaker enterprises would result.

With respect to the more immediate question of how to finance the transportation industry, it is clear that the barge line, motor carrier, and pipeline industries can finance themselves, but there is a real question as to whether the airlines and the railroads will be able to finance themselves in the years ahead. These two modes have the greatest capital requirements because of their normal capital intensiveness. In addition, because of the advent of a new generation of wide-body jets, the airline industry will have special financial needs. In the railroad industry, there may be additional needs if traffic increases as a result of its comparative energy efficiency. The removal of barriers to the formation of multimodal companies would not affect these problems at all. The airline industry and the railroad industry will have to solve their own financing problems over the next five years, irrespective of whether they get into other, more attractive ends of the transportation industry.

I am closer to the railroad industry than I am to the airline industry, but I think a good case can be made that the stronger railroads, the western railroads, are going to be able to meet their financing needs. The midwestern railroads will not, and the Conrail system, of course, is at the mercy of the federal government.

MR. BARNUM: I would like to ask Hays Watkins how he, as a railroad executive, would view this question if he were to consider going multimodal. Would the ability to raise capital be a factor in your consideration? Would it be a plus in that respect or a completely incidental consideration?

HAYS T. WATKINS, chairman and president, Chessie System, Inc.: From our standpoint, the financing would be the least of our concerns. To go back to what one of the other speakers said, the rate of return is really the key.

I would like, though, to take up a couple of things that Mr. Terry said. I have been puzzling over how it helps us to make money so that we pay taxes to the government to give money to Conrail, to buy equipment, to take business away from us. As for giving money to Conrail for a rate base, the railroads have not used rates of return or rate basis for pricing—

MR. TERRY: Operating ratio.

MR. WATKINS: I do not see how this would have any impact on the ability of the railroads to raise rates because, whether we like it or not, rate increases are primarily a response to competition with the other modes of transportation. So I would have to disagree with you that rail subsidy to Conrail helps the industry. I think it does just the reverse. At the appropriate time, some of us in the railroad industry must strongly and violently object to continuing subsidies to Conrail. I know, from our standpoint, we intend to pursue our objection vigorously.

Let me comment on the assertion that railroad retirement is subsidized by the federal government. This often-made claim is simply not correct. The railroad industry has been required by law to pay the cost of benefits received as a result of employment outside the industry. This inequity was corrected through legislation in 1974 that relieved railroads from part of the burden of paying in effect "dual benefits" in the case of employees who had worked outside the industry. This financing cannot remotely be equated to the outlay of billions of dollars for the construction and maintenance of waterway facilities or highway facilities used by rail competitors. Therefore, I would have to disagree that the railroads have been subsidized by the federal government. Perhaps shippers have been subsidized, and employees, but the railroads per se have not.

Over the long pull, it seems to me that the people who use a service or a product must pay for it, and this has to be the shippers or the users. It has been evident here today that the question is who pays what, and when. The users of any commodity or service—not just freight shippers—want to pay less than anyone else. If we can pay less than what is our fair share, whatever that might be, then we are ahead of the game. If we are in the position of paying more than our fair share, again, whatever that is, we are behind the eight ball. The railroads perceive that they are paying more than their fair share and that the other modes are paying less. Therefore the key to the whole problem, it seems, is to determine, first, what the costs are, and second, how we adjust or redress this imbalance, whatever it may be, over the short or the long term. This, obviously, would take a long series of studies, but I submit that this is something AEI should address and I think is addressing. Everybody has to pay for what they get before we ever arrive at the point where the railroad industry, the barge industry, the truck industry, or the transportation industry is paying—or earning—what it "should."

MR. BROWNE: I wonder if Mr. Low-Beer has an explanation as to why some railroads in the least dense traffic area are ten and twelve times more successful than other rail carriers in the heavy traffic area? I am sure that Southern Railway and Norfolk & Western are not in as dense an area as is Conrail, and yet their return is ten or twelve times better than that of the average railroad.

MR. LOW-BEER: There are always companies in every industry that are more profitable and some that are less profitable. One can look at the traffic base, at the yard operations, and at how many man-hours are put in to move a ton-mile, and one can find some answers. The main point, however, appears to be that to earn a rate of return which is, by any standard, mediocre requires an enormous effort in the railroad industry. The returns that I cite as being fair or mediocre in normal industrial companies would be terrific in the railroad industry.

MR. BARNUM: I would like to ask Mr. Romoff whether multimodal capability has ever been a factor in the Canadian experience. Although the Canadian Pacific probably does not have any problem raising capital, does the fact that a transportation company is multimodal enter into the calculus of investors in Canada? Does the presence of multimodal Canadian Pacific discourage the financing of a single mode company?

HARVEY M. ROMOFF, assistant vice president for corporate development, Canadian Pacific: Personally, I would suspect the answer is that that is not the case. Canadian Pacific is a large company with a long history, and for many years it has had no difficulty in finding capital.

Whether it is single modal or multimodal or diversified into many industries is of little importance in terms of financing.

MR. BARNUM: Is the presence of a multimodal company a deterrent to investing in single mode companies or would that be just speculation?

MR. ROMOFF: Speculation. If there is any difficulty, it is that CP is a very large company and certainly has access to all the capital markets. Many of the smaller companies undoubtedly find it more difficult to raise capital than does CP, but that is not because CP is diversified in transportation. This is not really a transportation issue.

Second Topic: If the statutory prohibitions were eliminated, what (if any) regulatory controls on multimodal ownership would be desirable?

MR. BARNUM: We turn now to the question of the appropriate regulation, if any, of multimodal ownership. The first discussant is the chairman of the ICC.

If we were to eliminate the statutory provisions in the Interstate Commerce Act and the Federal Aviation Act, which treat multimodal acquisition or entry questions differently from intramodal questions, would the antitrust laws plus the existing laws with respect to intramodal acquisitions be adequate? Would a different standard be desirable? If the existing standards were eliminated, would you simply go to the antitrust laws or would you want to retain in a regulatory agency some review over multimodal acquisitions?

A. DANIEL O'NEAL, JR., chairman, Interstate Commerce Commission: I feel a little uneasy discussing this whole subject. It is an issue that has been around for a long time, but, frankly, I have not paid much attention to it recently. This conference is certainly beneficial to me, personally, in that it has made me focus some attention on this issue. I am happy to be here at this stage, now that we have resolved the question as to whether multimodalism is a good idea. I gather we are at the implementation stage.

Because it is an uncertain area, I probably have a lot more questions than answers. I would start by assuming that we are talking only about a change in or elimination of the restrictions on multimodal ownership. To eliminate all restrictions would, of course, require statutory changes.

Some reduction of restrictions could occur without legislation. For example, the Interstate Commerce Commission might do a few things in the direction of allowing railroads to acquire motor carriers in cases where the motor carrier movement is subsequent to or prior to a rail movement. There was a review of the matter some years ago, within the commission. The Bureau of Economics did a quick study and concluded that there could be some changes by the commission through a rule-making proceeding. But nothing has occurred in that area. If there were no statutory changes in entry or in rate provisions, the acquisition of a motor carrier by a railroad—and I am talking principally about those two modes—could occur under Section 5 of the Interstate Commerce Act and would be undertaken in a way similar to an acquisition of one motor carrier by another today. I would not see any particular need to change that approach.

To obtain authority to acquire a motor carrier, a railroad would have to meet the test of public convenience and necessity (PC&N). This might be difficult if it is acquiring a motor carrier that provides service parallel to that of the railroad. It might be more difficult than, say, obtaining authority for motor carrier service of a collection and distribution nature in connection with a trailer-on-flatcar (TOFC) system.

There might be some reason to think about a change in the PC&N requirement if there were a change in the statutory policy. Of course, such a change would make it easier for the railroads to obtain motor carrier authority than for the motor carriers to obtain such additional authority. There might be substantial objection to that.

One matter that needs to be weighed is whether and to what extent there would be an effect on existing carriers. My guess is that, if intermodalism were advanced substantially, this process would divert traffic away from motor carriers. The motor carriers would not be happy about that, nor would the Teamsters. This is obviously a political problem that would have to be addressed.

A more important question might concern the interrelation among the regulatory bodies. What sort of coordination would be required among the agencies in the case of, for example, consolidations of air carriers and surface carriers or shipping companies and other carriers? Elimination of the restrictions in the statute would not necessarily require any greater coordination. I think coordination could be accomplished under the existing statutes.

There might possibly be a necessity for a joint approach. We do have a joint board mechanism on the statute books with the Civil Aeronautics Board, but it relates only to rate issues and to my knowledge it has never been used. We have nothing of that kind with the Federal Maritime Commission, and, again, I am not really sure it would be necessary.

I would sum up by saying that I am not sure, from a rather brief review, that the statutes governing the regulatory bodies would require any substantial change, other than the change necessary to ease the restrictions on multimodal development. I think the statutes adequately cover the kinds of issues that would arise—competition would be potentially a major one, although I have trouble finding that issue in these proposals.

LINDA KAMM, general counsel, U.S. Department of Transportation: In the year since I have been at DOT, nobody ever raised with me the question of multimodal ownership until John Barnum invited me to participate in this meeting. Since then I have had some opportunity to think about the question and to consider whether industry really perceives a need or an economy in multimodal ownership. I think the turnout here gives an indication that there is at least a great deal of interest in the subject.

One issue is the relationship between multimodal ownership and intermodal transportation. If we assume a need for more intermodal transportation, with concomitant benefits in fuel efficiency and in the shipper's ability to get one-stop service and to assign accountability for the shipment of a product, the question is whether multimodal ownership can introduce efficiencies that enhance the prospects for intermodal transportation.

We now obviously have a very complicated and anachronistic patchwork system. Rod Eyster's paper amply illustrates the confusion and notes that even where there are no statutory barriers to multimodal ownership, the economic regulatory agencies have often been reluctant to permit it. It is no longer clear, I think, what these various statutory and administrative prohibitions are designed to protect against. In some situations there is an interest in preserving competition among the acquired carriers, while in others the aim is to preserve competition among the acquiring carriers. While striving to attain a more flexible system we have to get a better idea, I think, of what forms multimodal ownership might take and what the problems might be in order to fashion, in that context, appropriate regulatory safeguards.

One potential concern is with discrimination. If a railroad owns a trucking company, for example, other truckers should not be adversely affected or disadvantaged in terms of handling goods or getting priority. Also in considering multimodal ownership, we will inevitably have to determine whether there should be additional flexibility in pricing and entry. As you know, the administration is moving to deregulate the air industry through pricing and entry flexibility. All-cargo aviation, of course, is already virtually deregulated. Surface transportation raises far greater problems, and in considering the possibility of greater multimodal ownership, we will need to look at ways to prevent monopoly abuse.

I suspect that most of these questions have not been analyzed recently, partly because there has been little indication of interest thus far. We will have to look into the matter in far greater detail when sufficient interest is shown.

MR. BARNUM: Chairman Kahn, having testified so effectively in some of the committees in Congress, will you now give us some of the benefit of your indoctrination in the transportation area?

ALFRED E. KAHN, chairman, Civil Aeronautics Board: I originally thought this seminar would give me an opportunity to learn what kinds of policies and problems we have at the board in this area. I think there is a lesson to be drawn from the fact that we all seem to have the same experience. It does not look as though anybody is banging on our doors, let alone knocking them down. So if you perceive a serious frustration of legitimate desires to engage in this kind of operation, your message is not getting across. I feel a little bit like the public opinion pollster who went around from door to door asking "Do you think the greater problem today is ignorance or apathy?" and one fellow answered "I don't know and I don't care."

After reading the three papers sent me [16] I emerged persuaded that, first, current market circumstances indicate that the patchwork of regulations we have today obviously was not designed in any integrated fashion and, second, the regulations that we have probably err on the side of excessive restrictionism because the historical evolution of these markets has certainly been in the direction of more effective intermodal competition. That is and will be particularly true in air transport, an area in which we are determined to move in a more liberal direction. The more effective competition is, intramodally and intermodally, the less logical basis there is for the kinds of restrictions that we have developed historically. I submit, however, that the original fears were not foolish. I read the Eyster paper as saying at times they were and at other times they were not.

In any event, I agree that even from the outset integration might have stimulated the exploitation of the possibilities of intermodal transportation. I read the paper on the Canadian experience by Mr. Romoff as saying the same thing. Trying to prove it, however, is like working with elaborate econometric exercises that invariably prove almost nothing except that it is hard to deny the clear evidence of your eyes. Historically, it seems clear to Mr. Romoff and to me that intermodal ownership motivated a greater development of intermodal operations in Canada than in this country—even though, as he points out, there are many differences between the two markets that help explain the differences in practices.

I have no difficulty with the general proposition that continuing flat prohibition of integration does not make any more sense in the

---

[16] Presented in Part I, above.

present market context than it does in industry generally. The burden of proof really ought to be on the people who argue in particular circumstances that intermodal ownership has, in fact, had deleterious effects or will have them. We do not prohibit vertical integration generally in the economy at large, and it seems to me that the same legal principle should apply to the increasingly competitive transportation industry.

Even though it is hard for me to see an enormous demonstrated need or demand for it, suppose we were to establish the same possibility of integration in the transportation field as we have in industry generally. What dangers should we be looking for? The only way I can answer is to ask, What was it we were worried about in the past? One fear was that when one mode exerted control over an acquired mode intermodal competition would be suppressed. The second fear was that the diversion of business might have a distorting effect on competition within one or another of the integrated fields. People have been talking about these fears for seventy-five years, and I cannot summarize them any better than the papers you have before you. They indicate what we should look for.

As Linda Kamm suggests, we should hold ourselves open to complaints of discriminatory treatment by nonintegrated carriers in either of the two fields and complaints about market foreclosure or unequal access to the facilities of the other mode. In addition, we should keep an eye on the respective market shares in the two areas. That is, are the integrated carriers getting increasing control over the acquired markets? I realize there is a certain arbitrariness about deciding which is the acquired, which is the acquiring. We should, presumably, look at both. Is there some tendency for an increased share of the market to fall into the hands of the integrated carriers? If we find that there is such a tendency, it does not necessarily mean that we should therefore disallow intermodalism; obviously the observed trend could merely reflect the efficiency advantages of integration. But at least that kind of evidence would answer the threshold question: Have the fears materialized?

For a first-cut answer, I turned to the one decision in the area by the CAB that I knew about before I came to the board—and what I knew about the airline industry before then would fill closets. I had read the decision back in the late 1960s when the CAB for the first time permitted long-haul surface carriers to go into the airfreight forwarding business. I had by chance devoted considerable attention to it in the second volume of my *Economics of Regulation*.[17] I also discovered that since then the board has had an inquiry to see what has happened in the interim.

---

[17] Alfred E. Kahn, *The Economics of Regulation: Principles and Institutions,* 2 vols. (New York: John Wiley & Sons, Inc., 1970).

If I may, I will read you a few of the things that the CAB found in this rather limited area—the only significant decision that I was able to discover in my not very extensive research. The administrative law judge concluded that "experience under the monitored entry program has shown that none of the evils predicted by the original opponents, namely the airlines and the independent forwarders, has materialized. The surface affiliations of the monitored entrants, the integrated carriers, have not had an adverse effect on the independent forwarders or on the industry."

He observed, "Twenty affiliated forwarders have received authority under the monitored entry program, but most never commenced operation." And only eight have survived. The number of independent forwarders, on the other hand, has grown from less than 200 to more than 330 in a period of seven years. "None of the affiliated forwarders has been able seriously to challenge Emery, who is one of the big opponents"—for obvious reasons—"UPS or Airborne, the independent forwarders which continue to dominate the industry.

"The five largest independents earn well over one half of the domestic forwarding revenues . . ." and so forth. "Moreover, although some diversion has resulted from the presence of surface carriers in the market, such diversion is not as significant as that caused by other independent forwarders. Moreover, the diversion did not arise from unfair competitive practices, such as 'piracy' "—they had the decency to put "piracy" in quotes—"of personnel or predatory rate making, nor does the record establish diversion of traffic from air to surface"— that is the feared suppression of the acquired carriers—"because of conflicts of interest in the surface carriers."

The administrative law judge also found it significant that a "number of tangible benefits have resulted from surface carrier participation in airfreight forwarding. First, the board's monitored entry program has permitted financially stable enterprises, committed to airfreight, to enter the industry. As a result, an industry characterized by heavy concentration and a few leaders"—this is an interesting case; it was the nonintegrated firms with a large share of the market that objected to this entry—"has received sorely needed competitive stimulus.

"Second, the record supports the conclusion that the largest of the surviving monitored entrants"—those would be the integrated ones— "have made significant progress in bringing new service to outlying areas, although their surface affiliations cannot be counted as the causative factor.

"The railroad affiliates have also provided air cargo service to many small hubs, and this expansion can be attributed to their surface affiliation. Third, the participation of surface forwarders has also generated new traffic, to some extent, by diverting surface business to air, which was one of the expectations." If truckers are given the right to go into this business, it would be expected that they might then have an incentive to develop it.

"It is important that the affiliated forwarders have had a positive rather than a negative impact upon the body of traffic handled by airfreight forwarders and direct air carriers.

"Thus, in varying degree, affiliated carriers have supplied their forwarders with financing, quality management, sophisticated communication and computer systems and equipment, opened up cities other than the largest traffic centers, provided new traffic from air shippers, new shippers by air, some intermodal activity, some service to hinterland points, and some diversion of surface traffic to air." [18]

The board therefore concluded that the experiment was a modest success and that the dangers had not materialized, but it said it would continue to look at the situation. And that is about what I would propose we do. I do not have an opinion—other than a bureaucratic one—about whether the surveillance job should go to the Antitrust Division or stay within the CAB. I really do not care. I would be perfectly happy if the job were in Mr. Seiden's hands because I trust his hands almost as much as I trust mine. I think that continued scrutiny is desirable, but I am undecided whether it need be more intensive than it is in industry generally now.

MR. BARNUM: You appear, at least, to be open to the option to review the flat prohibition against acquisition of an air carrier certificate, whether the review be in your hands or Elliott Seiden's at the Antitrust Division. You have not seen any of those cases because there has been no basis for making application for a certificate.

MR. KAHN: Precisely. My point is that I cannot see anybody from the air industry dominating the trucking industry and suppressing competition in trucking. The ICC does such a good job, nobody else is needed to suppress competition—though I know Dan O'Neal is trying. Nor do I see trucking firms concentrating control in the air cargo business, particularly with free entry. If there is free entry in one line and free entry in the other line, who cares? But I am willing to continue to look at the question.

MR. BARNUM: Elliott Seiden of the Antitrust Division, whose capable hands have just been described, is going to offer some views on this issue.

---

[18] The preceding quotations are from the *Long-Haul Motor/Railroad Carrier and Freight Forwarder Authority Case*, Docket no. 26907 et al., initial decision of E. Robert Seaver, administrative law judge, October 22, 1975, as cited in the opinion of the CAB, June 27, 1977.

ELLIOTT M. SEIDEN, chief, Transportation Section, Antitrust Division, U.S. Department of Justice: We have all just heard a very solid preview of what I was going to say from one of the best antitrust lawyers I know, Chairman Kahn. The question is whether traditional antitrust analysis would be sufficient to meet any anticompetitive problems that might arise from reducing the artificial barriers to cross-modal ownership that now exist. I think the answer is yes, and I think it is a fairly simple answer to reach. It can be approached in two ways. As David Munro indicated, intermodal ownership can arise from either merger, acquisition, or internal expansion. I think it is fairly easy to conclude that traditional analysis under Section 7 of the Clayton Act would permit a reasonable determination of whether a particular acquisition or merger was going to be anticompetitive and whether it should be challenged under the antitrust laws.[19]

I should add, parenthetically, that the phrase "antitrust laws" might not be appropriate in this seminar because we are discussing the possibility of removing only the specific and unique controls applicable to cross-modal ownership and not all regulatory control over mergers and acquisitions. I assume that Section 408 of the Federal Aviation Act would still be in existence, as well as the Interstate Commerce Act. It therefore might be more appropriate to talk about antitrust analysis rather than antitrust laws. But since Clayton 7 ordinarily plays a significant role in traditional agency analysis of mergers and acquisition, it is fairly safe to proceed along this line.

A cross-modal acquisition could present horizontal or vertical problems. A horizontal problem would exist, for example, if a long-haul trucker were competing directly with a long-haul railroad for the exact same kinds of traffic. In that circumstance, traditional analysis of the product market and the geographical market would be easy to make and easy to attack under Clayton 7 either in the courts or before the agencies, if appropriate. The more obvious kind of competitive problem that would arise under cross-modal ownership would be vertical. Here the courts have provided more than sufficient analysis—in terms of clogs on the market system, as the Supreme Court has said, or market foreclosure, as Chairman Kahn said—to determine fairly easily whether there are anticompetitive problems. Therefore I do not see any problem in determining whether cross-modal ownership is attackable under traditional antitrust analysis. I think it clearly is.

Another way to get cross-modal ownership, as Mr. Munro pointed out, is through internal expansion. In the transportation industry,

---

[19] Section 7 of the Clayton Act (1914), as amended, 15 U.S.C. § 18, prohibits the acquisition of stock or assets of another corporation when the effect "may be substantially to lessen competition, or to tend to create a monopoly," in any line of commerce in any section of the country.

internal expansion is possible usually only by acquiring a certificate from an agency. That is not entirely true because, as far as I can tell, a certificate is not needed from the Federal Maritime Commission to become an ocean carrier, and it therefore might be possible for a railroad to expand into ocean shipping simply by buying some ships. In the case of certification, however, the question is whether traditional PC&N analysis should still apply. Since the Antitrust Division, along with Chairman Kahn, is not at all convinced that certificates of public convenience and necessity are the best way to allow entry into transportation industries, I cannot today argue in favor of continuing to use these certificates. But if certificates are going to be used, it would seem to me that the agencies could easily handle entry into the various modes under traditional PC&N analysis without too much concern about the unique anticompetitive problems applicable to cross-modal situations.

MR. BARNUM: Tom Allison in his years at the Senate Commerce Committee has dealt with some of these problems of regulation of transportation, and I would like to have his views on how to control multimodalism, whether in the context of entry or of a merger.

THOMAS G. ALLISON, counsel, Senate Committee on Appropriations, and former chief counsel, Senate Committee on Commerce, Science, and Transportation: I have some concern as to whether direct applicability of the antitrust laws is the most appropriate mechanism for dealing with possible market abuse by an intermodal carrier. For example, one can point to the relative lack of success of the antitrust laws in controlling economic concentration in nonregulated industries.

There may be good public policy reasons for doing things that the antitrust laws would not necessarily reach. For example, fuel efficiency and other public policy goals may well be served through some continuing role for a regulatory agency when the same results could not be obtained by simple strict application of the antitrust laws. Whatever the role of the regulatory agencies, I would hope that the notion of regulated competition could be applied broadly enough to include such things as product competition, even where that would be a substitute for transportation. The market dominance test comes to mind.

The practical political problems would be substantial in attempting to move toward intermodal ownership with the kind of evidence we currently have—in other words, in attempting to eliminate the barriers that Rod Eyster's paper identified. It may well be that, as a practical matter, one would want to proceed step by step. Perhaps primary consideration could be given to eliminating controls over the acquisition and operation of motor carrier service by railroads whenever there is an intervening line-haul rail movement. This would be something Congress could possibly address piecemeal in the current motor carrier regulatory debate, and it might also give us some valuable experience in an area where many congressmen believe there has not been sufficient growth—the use of trailer on flatcar and container on flatcar.

There is a great deal of interest in this issue in the Senate in general and in the commerce committee in particular. Russell Long, among others, is a strong proponent of multimodal ownership, and his chairmanship of the subcommittee would help in that area. This proceeding may help to focus the debate to a point at which specific proposals can emerge, possibly similar to the one I have suggested with respect to the motor carriers.

MR. BARNUM: I would like to ask William Jarrel Smith, deputy managing director of the Federal Maritime Commission, if he has some observations to add to this regulatory question.

WILLIAM JARREL SMITH, JR., deputy managing director, Federal Maritime Commission: Basically, the FMC has no restrictions on whether there can be integration and ownership between different modes. We have not prohibited any such activity, and in fact we have seen it occur from time to time.

There was mention earlier of the experience of American Export Lines in going into various modes. We do not have any statutory problems with that; our statutes encourage people to come into U.S. trades. We have no limitations on entry. The international ocean trades are open to anyone who wants to provide a service and who meets certain minimum obligations of filing tariffs and meeting certain requirements, for example, with respect to oil pollution. These carriers can come into our trades and we're glad to have them. We have competition in our trades. Other segments of transportation, such as railroads and trucking companies, have come into our trades under the guise of non-vessel-operating common carriers. They file tariffs with us and we are glad to have them. We have competition in our trades and complete freedom for all people to come in.

One thing that has not been mentioned here but that I think is important is international trade. We have numerous non-U.S.-flag operators that are incorporated under foreign laws and that have integrated their operations in foreign countries. When U.S.-flag companies compete with these people they are faced with operations that are different from our own. It is important to realize that in the international sector American transportation companies are in competition with people who have freedom under their own national laws in Europe or in the Far East to do what they want to do or what they are able to do. We should recognize that our own domestic antitrust or regulatory laws sometimes do not fit this international situation very well.

This point is certainly important to the FMC and to U.S.-flag carriers operating internationally.

MR. HILTZHEIMER: As the regulatory agency is probably aware, almost a year ago I got together with some of the rails and truckers to talk about the need for better consultation between the ocean carriers governed by the Shipping Act and the motor carriers and railroads under the ICC. We in the ocean carriage business wanted to have an ocean carrier rate conference and be able to talk to a motor carrier or a rate bureau. Right now antitrust laws do not permit that. Intermodalism is a fact of life; it started in the 1960s and, particularly in the United States, has grown very quickly. But we have a kind of fragmented pricing effort taking place in a vacuum, sometimes instituted by foreign ocean carriers who are not really familiar with the cost economics of land transportation. There is no ability at present for the kind of close coordination and consultation and rate making on through rates between ocean and land that we think we need. That would obviously benefit the shipper, probably as much or more than multimodal ownership.

As I said earlier, there are no statutory prohibitions at the moment that I can think of that would prohibit an ocean carrier from moving into ownership of railroad or truck line or what have you. Our position would be that the discretion of the regulatory agency, if any, should be broad enough to permit the evolution of multimodal ownership if that is what companies decide they want. I mentioned that Sea-Land at the moment would not necessarily be interested in that.

One other factor—I think the secretary mentioned it at lunch—is the cost of fuel. I have done a study, and as far as our industry is concerned there are all kinds of scenarios as to what fuel is going to cost in 1985. According to the worst scenario, that of the Chase Manhattan Bank—and we hope that does not apply—the cost of bunker fuel in our business will be 100 percent higher in 1985 than it is today. There will be very little change in the capital cost per ton-mile or the operating cost per ton-mile, but the fuel cost per ton-mile will be so high under that scenario that in my view we would have trouble extracting the difference in cost from the trade—that is, from the shipper that pays the freight, the consumer.

If that is a true assessment of the future, there would be a very definite, dramatic change in ocean carriage, and the number of ships crossing the ocean would decrease substantially. The carriers with the largest capacity—that is, the capability to move the largest number of containers or the largest amount of freight with one power plant—would have the economic wherewithal to stand that situation, and those with small ships would have such high fuel costs that they would disappear in a hurry.

This scenario needs to be translated for domestic transportation. As Secretary Adams indicated at lunch, he is concerned about what might happen in this country to the petroleum-oriented transportation industry if fuel costs go up dramatically. We have not really thought about what would happen, that is, how we would then move our goods. I do not have any answers, but I think it is an area that we ought to address. Rising fuel costs may be the single most important thing that forces a change in transportation as we know it today.

MR. BARNUM: I think Ken McLaughlin mentioned joint rates and through rates earlier in another context, and it occurs to me that he might want to try out this problem with Chairman O'Neal. Here is a company that is multimodal in some respects but is not now able to take advantage of that fact because of regulatory or statutory limitations on through rates. Have I interpreted your earlier remarks correctly?

MR. MCLAUGHLIN: The Interstate Commerce Commission has supported our position, and in their presentation to Congress every year has recommended that that portion of the law be changed. Unfortunately, Congress has not acted upon it.

MR. O'NEAL: Maybe we should address that question to Tom Allison.

MR. ALLISON: As I recall, the Senate did do that.

MR. BARNUM: Is there any consideration of through rates in the House? Bill Druhan from the Interstate and Foreign Commerce Committee is going to tell us it is a problem for Public Works.

WILLIAM T. DRUHAN, staff director, House Subcommittee on Transportation and Commerce: It is a real problem in the House because of the jurisdictions of the different committees. One of the problems that you did not touch on with regard to regulation is a political problem. No pun intended, but we have to get our house in order and settle the jurisdictional matter.

MR. BARNUM: Fred Rooney did mention it in his remarks earlier.

MR. DRUHAN: In direct answer to your question, there is little we can do now. It is a frustrating problem. You recall the subcommittee had a panel similar to this one last December. Similar matters were brought up as to what is going on, and complaints were made by the shippers and the railroads about the 4R Act [Railroad Revitalization and Regulatory Reform Act of 1976] and the lack of regulatory reform. We got no answers. All we know is that we failed with the 4R Act. It did not result in any regulatory reform. The problem is still there. Some say the act was poorly written, but we say it was poorly administered; others say that there was no problem. The shippers think it's great, the railroads think it's terrible, and it reminds me of 1974. We have not made any progress. So where are we going from here? The problem of through rates and joint rates is similar to the argument we had with buses and Amtrak. Where is the intermodalism? Each one points a finger at the other. We are looking for some kind of conclusions reached by groups such as this so that we can take some kind of action on those matters.

MR. O'NEAL: I cannot let Bill Druhan's comment go without saying something. He sells himself too short. The Congress did take important action in passing the 4R Act, and I think that the Interstate Commerce Commission has faithfully fulfilled the policy that was laid out in the act. If there are any questions about that, I certainly would want to go before the Congress and talk it out. A lot of loose comments have been made about whether the railroads have actually been able to use the 4R Act provisions, particularly the rate flexibility provisions, but since there have not been many filings we do not know much. Where there have been filings under the act, there is yet to be a suspension. There have been a few investigations, but those rates have gone into effect.

There have also been some rate adjustments under the seasonal rate provision; the southern carriers put in a 20 percent rate increase not long ago that sailed right by. In earlier times, it would have been investigated and probably suspended.

We said in our report to the Congress that it is a little early to tell, and this view was shared by the Department of Transportation. The act has been in effect since October 1976, but there have not yet been many filings under the act. I would think that before Congress makes adjustments it ought to require the railroads to show that the thing is not working. And they cannot show it unless they give it a try.

I want to put it on the record that I agree with the comments of the Antitrust Division. I also want to say something about what Tom Allison mentioned. If I understand correctly, he would propose some legislative action that would require a rail movement somewhere in the process, either prior to or subsequent to the motor carrier. That may be something that could be done administratively within the agency. Indeed, it is the very thing that the Bureau of Economics suggested in 1970. I am not saying we are about to initiate something like that, and, judging from the comments by Mr. Romoff, I am not sure those restrictions would be helpful or would result in improved use of trailer on flatcar. That, I think, would be an open question.

MR. DRUHAN: I think you misinterpreted me. You were adequately represented up there by yourself, and Commissioner Betty Jo Christian made the same comment that nobody filed. Railroads responded by saying, "Why file if we know what the answer is going to be?" The fallacy, they say, is in the act, and the point remains that nothing has happened. Whether it is good or bad that nothing happens, that was not the intent of Congress. We are not going to take precipitate action—you know us better than that. If we take any action it will be amazing, but it certainly will not be precipitate. There will be adequate time to explain why nothing has happened, but I think everybody should agree that nothing has happened.

MR. WILLIAM K. SMITH: I would like to get in between on this one. A half dozen or so of the 4R Act pricing provisions and the basic argument between railroads and shippers that you refer to concern market dominance more than anything else. I agree with what the chairman was saying. There have been some rate filings and some requests for the ICC to suspend the rate change requests. Something like nine out of ten of the requests to suspend have been knocked down, or maybe 100 percent of them. I have been telling this to some of my pricing friends at the railroads. I think they are really missing a bet. Sitting back and saying nothing is going to happen I think is a real mistake on the pricing part of the railroad industry. It is very difficult, as intended in that act, to get a suspension. Almost two years have gone by, and I think a lot of things could have been asked for. A lot of shippers could have said, "I protest, suspend it." But the tariff or rate would have gone through because the shipper cannot meet all the tests required for a suspension. A lot has happened, but I think a lot more could have happened—not in reference to market dominance but in the whole context of suspensions. A number of suspensions were filed. General Mills probably filed as many as any one source, and I think we have been clobbered on all of them and that is the way it is supposed to be. We could not meet those tests in our allegations.

MR. DRUHAN: One of the problems that this symposium will bring out is that there was no coordination between the modes with regard to the regulations. They were isolated on the issue. In the case of General Mills, shipping might not be a problem, and with shipments of coal or grain there is no problem, but there is in other cases the secretary was alluding to. But we were not interrelating the problems that the railroads have with those of the other modes, and there is no coordinating regulation within the government, which is probably where we should start.

Summary and Conclusions

MR. BARNUM: I asked Hays Watkins—and this was presumptive of me, but I have a high regard for his ability to analyze and to state an issue succinctly—if he would open our final session with a summary of what he has heard and learned today and any observations he may want to add. I have asked John Terry to do the same, and we will have time, when they have concluded, to let anybody else who wants to offer some remarks.

MR. WATKINS: It would be rather presumptuous of me, particularly since I am in the railroad industry, after all the comments today about railroads, to try to summarize in five or ten minutes a full day of comments by the secretary of transportation, the chairman of the Interstate Commerce Commission, the chairman of the Civil Aeronautics Board, and other industry and government and labor leaders. Instead, I would like to give a few comments and a few notes that I have jotted down, perhaps as a basis for further thought, either collectively or individually.

I wrote down three questions. First, are there intermodal companies or multimodal companies? The answer, obviously, is yes, in varying degrees and varying configurations which we have heard about today.

The second question is, are there barriers to multimodal ownership? The answer to that one, obviously, is yes, there are barriers. In most cases they are not insurmountable; in some cases they are real; in other cases they may be more apparent than real.

The third question is, has the time come to reassess this entire question? I have been struck by the generally constructive spirit exhibited by all the comments today. It has been obvious that representatives of certain modes are more favorably disposed than representatives of other modes or labor groups. Nevertheless, running all through the comments today is a generally optimistic attitude that the time has come at least to review the problem. There seems to be general agreement that the series of regulations and restrictions and congressional acts, while they may have served a purpose at the time they were enacted, now in hindsight appear to be more of a jerry-built series of individual actions rather than a sound foundation of transportation policy for a nation such as the United States.

With the optimistic or affirmative answers to these three questions, the next one is, how do we proceed? One of the first things we have to do is to define the problem or, perhaps, define the need. There seems to be general agreement that this problem should be reviewed, but we have not specifically defined the problem or the need. Perhaps that would be too much to hope for in one day.

We must recognize, obviously, the differing views of the various groups here. We must discuss the alternatives, and we must determine the benefits to be received or the problems to be encountered. Then we can begin what I would term the political process of accommodating the differing views of the various groups, to see what is both desirable and possible.

The problem was discussed in the three provocative advance papers. All of us owe a great debt of gratitude to the three gentlemen who prepared these papers, and I thought they offered a very good preparation for today.

Certainly, the problem is interesting and intriguing, but it is obviously not critical. Time and again the comment has been made that the problem is not crying out for a solution that must be found tomorrow. Perhaps that is good, because for one reason or another we have accommodated ourselves to the situation. We have learned either to live with it or to work around it or to wire through it. On the other hand, we have realized that it can be a problem.

Our comments here have been, basically, from a short-range standpoint. Perhaps we should see where the problem or the situation is leading us. Perhaps the short-range problems are only a hint of the things to come five, ten, and twenty years from now. I would hope that out of these discussions could come some effort toward a long-range solution. First, what is the problem; then, what is the goal—how do we get from here to there?

One of the many very interesting conflicts that struck me is the question of economy of scale versus the smallness to react quickly to customer needs. I can argue, as I am sure all of you can, on both sides of the fence. But this is not a problem that can be resolved, and the mere fact of multimodal ownership may, in fact, slow down the reaction process and thus offset any benefits to the shipping public or to the stockholders.

Another question concerns free market operation versus regulatory control. Some of us would like to have the luxury of trying things in a completely free market. We would like to see if we know how to run our businesses better than the regulatory groups that tell us what to do and how to do it. But, obviously, that is a luxury we will not have. It is politically unfeasible, impossible. But the issue of free market versus regulation has been raised.

Another one is the question of the "institution," particularly in the railroad industry. The institutionalized organization—the ponderous machine, as I call it—is seen in conflict with the ability to use innovation and ingenuity. Here again, we get into small versus big: the larger the institution, the older, and the more institutionalized, the less it is able to adjust. This may be one of the problems with the railroad industry. I knew we had a lot of them, and I have heard a few more today.

We also have the question of overall control, master planning, or monopoly versus the profit center. In the illustration of the Canadian Pacific, the organization first operated for the benefit of the whole and was subsequently divided into profit centers with at least semiautonomy if not relatively complete autonomy. I think we must recognize this as a key lesson when we get into the area of multimodal activity.

I was also struck by the stated perceptions of railroads—and here my background comes out. I try to be objective generally, but here I cannot be. The perception of the railroads by the general public is one thing, but the attitude within this group is something else. You perceive the railroads as a powerful monopoly, an all-encompassing thing that needs controlling—I didn't realize we were quite that bad. For a group of educated, informed transportation people to come out with this idea surprises and, frankly, appalls me.

We have also, today, touched the question whether the profit opportunity of the transportation companies is better under multimodal ownership or diversification outside the railroad industry. While some of us in the railroad industry may be inept, I cannot conceive that everyone in the railroad industry is inept to the extent that our industry rate of return is low and the truck and the barge line rates of return are high. There must be something, other than management, that affects us. I would like to think so, anyway, but perhaps, again, this is subjective rather than objective. But we must examine the question of what it is about the railroad industry that makes it relatively less profitable than other forms of transportation. Is it that we are institutionalized, that we are too big, that we are overregulated, that we are living in the past century, or that the public perceives us to be living in the past century and gauges us accordingly? There must be something there.

Perhaps it is a question of more equitable user charges or more equitable payments for the goods and services that we use. Again, we talk about regulation; we are all against regulation—except as it affects us. We are for motherhood and the flag and against sin in most forms, unless it affects us. In other words, our attitude is to take a strong offense in running our business, but we want regulation there to protect us. We want to have the ability to go out and do what we can, but, in case things go wrong, we want something to hide behind. We ask for freedom from regulation, but we want the protection of regulation, too.

We also have the question of evolutionary changes versus major change by legislation, regulation, or management, or the lack of change in any of them. I have to say that dialogues such as this hasten the evolutionary process, which, in my opinion, is the only way that any change in multimodal ownership or, indeed, in any coordinated transportation activities can occur.

The question has come up whether a multimodal organization would operate as separate profit centers or as one unit, and there have been various comments about the overwhelming power of such multi-

157

modal giants. Those concerns have been adequately discussed, and I think that perhaps we are tilting at windmills. There are existing anti-trust laws. There are the "pure" laws of economics which indicate that a big organization is not necessarily an efficient one. We have the results of the Canadian lines, some of the airlines, and the water lines here that have found separate profit centers to be advantageous.

In the final analysis, the shippers or the users have to pay the bill for whatever transportation or other services are provided. Shippers like competition because it gives them the ability to play one mode against the other. To the extent that all modes are under one company, however, the flexibility of shippers' use of the competitive process is reduced. On the other hand, competition has made this country great, and I hope it will continue to make this country great.

There is no question in my mind that there is still too much physical plant in the railroad industry. If I thought that multimodal ownership would enable us to get rid of these duplicating branch lines and the secondary main lines, I would be all for it. But I am not persuaded that that would, in fact, be the response.

I cannot resist commenting on Secretary Adams's concern about energy. I agree with him completely that we must find more energy-efficient ways of moving our freight. But, as a railroader, I do not find it logical that Congress appropriates money to repair potholes and refuses to consider the subject of user charges.

MR. TERRY: The two modes that are having some difficulty, the rail mode and the freight forwarders, say they want more freedom, and the two modes that are doing better financially, the trucks and the water carriers, tend to want protection. Perhaps the very success of their modes argues against the need for protection.

I am not worried about any rail competition, and I am in the trucking business and have been for a while. Nor do I think that truckers need any protection from railroads or freight forwarders. What I really worry about, as a trucker, is the things that may happen to us as the railroads move closer to that chasm that I think they are approaching. We know that railroads have 1.8 percent return on investment, and, as Hays Watkins said earlier, it is modal competition, not the ICC, that is holding down their rates. Those two things mean that the railroads are consuming their assets.

We know that inflation is more than 1.8 percent and that the rails are facing big problems of rail and tie replacement and of maturing low-cost debt. It is therefore logical to assume that more railroads are going to be queuing up before the bankruptcy court as did the Penn Central, the Milwaukee, and the Rock Island. I think that holds a risk for the truckers—obviously, not as much risk as for the railroads themselves, but much more risk for the truckers than does a somewhat eased regulation of railroads that would allow them to be more flexible.

We have to look at the specific proposal: Since the real intermodal restrictions are on railroads—except for the one on freight forwarders, which is also very real—should we permit the rails to own other modes of transportation that they cannot now own, such as motor carriers? I, personally, am much interested in things that will help the railroads stay in the private sector, without federal assistance, and I cannot help but look at this proposal in that light.

In the last couple of years, we at IU have done a great deal of work analyzing our market share because we think that marketing is going to be important in the trucking business. We know what our share is of all the for-hire general freight markets from state to state. And we know that 2 percent is a good market share—we rarely get above 10 percent; 30 percent is unheard of.

As I mentioned earlier, the map in Professor Roberts's paper was very persuasive. It shows that in order for the rail piggyback service to reach the threshold, they have to gain very large shares of all the freight on an intercity pair, both the private and regulated traffic. I asked myself, "If I were a railroader and I could buy a truck line, would I want to do it?" I concluded that if I were trying to get the share I needed on one of these city pairs—say, Los Angeles to Dallas, which has eighteen loads a day—I would have to get all those loads to make a viable piggyback service. Would I buy a certificate to run from Los Angeles to Dallas, which would cost a great deal for the certificate alone, or would I try to get the freight forwarders and the private carriers (who, by the way, represent more than half the intercity freight) to put their freight on my service? For-hire carriers not tied up by Teamster union restrictions might also put some freight on piggyback. No, I do not think I would buy that motor carrier. I would try to be merely the line-haul carrier and get their freight on my railroad. I do not think that intermodal ownership will help rails very much.

I have another problem with intermodal ownership. If we do not find some way to turn the rail industry around before those ties have to be replaced and before those bonds come due, then it stands to reason that the federal government will have to do something. It probably means some form of support such as the Rock Island and Conrail now receive. When that happens, I do not want the railroad that is getting support to own a motor carrier. I am not afraid to compete with any railroad, but I do not want to compete with the federal government and I do not take it lightly. We run a European trucking company, and in Sweden we compete with ASG, the truck line owned by the Swedish national railroads; in France we compete with Calberson, the truck line owned by the French national railroad. Shenker, the second largest freight forwarder in the world—only Kuhn and Nagel is bigger—is owned by the German state railroad. And we all know that in Britain the government transportation companies are all over the place, including National Carriers which competes with us—again, a government-owned entity, taking government money. Because I do not want to compete with the government, I do not want to see any government money go to railroads that operate motor carriers.

The prospect of federal assistance to railroad owners of motor carriers really troubles me. Since I do not see that intermodal ownership would do much to help the rail problem, the prospect of federal support for railroads in the trucking business swings me against intermodal ownership for the railroads. I believe it is in the interest of my business to take some chances on regulatory changes that would help the rails avoid any kind of a collapse. Speeding up the deregulatory process would help. The fact that there are fourteen transcontinental truckers and no transcontinental railroads makes a pretty good case for regulatory change. I am very much for things that will help the rails stay alive and stay in the private sector. But I do not think permitting intermodal ownership is one that does much to help.

I think the major problem in the freight business is the slow rate of innovation, the rate of progress. The industry, including the trucking sector, is very slow to change. To the extent that regulation impedes change, it is not good. But I do not agree that we need easier entry. In the trucking business there are already two certificated carriers for every load of freight on a city pair. And let's face it, to be reasonably efficient, we would like to have at least one full truck every day. I therefore do not want to go toward deregulation the way the air people have. I do not think it has been beneficial, and certainly it has not done anything about stopping the concentration in the airfreight business.

We must find a way to promote innovation, and we must do something about the rail industry before we have to compete with government railroads here as we do in Europe. I do not want that to happen.

MR. LOW-BEER: One of the major problems in this discussion is that we all take the view that we do not want our own personal ox to be gored. In all these problems, the tendency is to seek a political solution that is relatively simple to implement. As an investor, I worry that these so-called solutions very often depend not on an accurate analysis of the fundamental issues, but on what is politically most feasible. We can analyze ad infinitum, but the results will not be very useful unless political consequences are considered. It is easy to assume that the truckers are profitable because they get a nice subsidy. But I do not know whether that is correct. It should be analyzed. I think we also ought to worry about who is going to put this $50 to 70 billion into the highway system. That is a lot of money.

Again, I emphasize that we should all be very careful about making dispassionate solutions when, in effect, our individual solutions and analysis reflect our own self-interest.

MR. TERRY: When I am not pursuing my continuing interest in transportation, I occasionally act as a lawyer on other matters. Last week I happened to be reading some of the files of IBM, a very well-managed company in the economy. For internal use, they have prepared an extremely intelligent, well-reasoned projection of conditions in the United States for the next five years. One sentence in particular struck me: "There will be continuing inability to reach agreement on fundamental issues."

MR. BARNUM: Well, we have another half hour to reach agreement.

PAUL O. ROBERTS, director, Center for Transportation Studies, Massachusetts Institute of Technology: Hays Watkins mentioned that there were no problems crying out for solution, and I would agree that this is the case except, perhaps, for the one that John Terry mentioned of how to keep the railroads from falling into the chasm. I would prefer to look at this issue as an opportunity, crying out for someone to step into it, rather than as a problem that must be solved. It is fairly evident around the table today, however, that some people do not want others to step into this opportunity, so there are two sides to the issue.

As for having to compete with government, Tom Browne's organization, United Parcel Service, delights in continuing to have government to compete with. Maybe they are the only ones around the table that do.

MR. BROWNE: Only when it is fair competition.

MR. ROBERTS: Is the post office fair competition?

Let me just say a couple of words about my background paper and two specific exhibits, Table 2 and Figure 8, blow-ups of which were distributed this morning. The point I was trying to make is that the U.S. markets are very thin. Truckers have learned how to deal with thin markets. Railroads, in their own way, as early as the Civil War, have learned how to deal with them. And they both deal with them in totally different ways.

The key to attacking a multimodal problem is in knowing how to deal with thin markets. It is necessary to aggregrate them to get the volumes up. The multimodal question becomes one of a trade-off between distance on the one hand and traffic density on the other. To offer multimodal services over short distances requires very high densities. In the long-distance markets the volumes can be much less, but it is necessary to get volume and to keep the costs down in doing it.

Table 2 and Figure 8 are meant to convey the essence of the problem, not the exact details. On the matrix (Table 2) I do not trust

161

the numbers as far as I can throw them, but they are from the U.S. government's census of transportation, which is the only published record we have of these intercity freight flows. They are riddled with disclosure problems and have to be taken with a grain of salt. Total flows are shown for each market in trucks per day, but only for manufacturing; agriculture, mining, and wholesale and retail distribution are not included. Only the trucking flows are shown. The TOFC markets are not broken out because the census of transportation shows only rail as a whole. We certainly need a new set of figures, and we need them as quickly as we can get them.

The figures on the map (Figure 8) are the threshold volumes as defined in my paper—that is, either traffic is dense enough to qualify, or the distance is long enough, or there is a combination of the two. Multimodal ownership could lower costs by eliminating some of the pickup and delivery charges, and aggregating markets would raise the densities. The map therefore does not necessarily show the way the world would be after multimodal ownership. Nor should it be taken as the reason multimodalism will not work; it may be, but we have to get better figures before we can say that definitely.

One last comment I might make is that there is a difference between multimodal operations, multimodal ownership, and multimodal management, and I think that we have to distinguish very carefully the ways in which we deal with each. One does not follow after another.

MR. SCHAEFER: I would like to tag onto Hays Watkins's comments and also Secretary Brock Adams's comments earlier about where we are today and where we are going tomorrow. Most of the discussion today touched on immediate problems; only a little of the future was discussed.

Our country has an opportunity in that we are becoming more international. Emery has seen very tough competition overseas. We have "toughed it out" in those markets and succeeded, which is one reason for supporting a more open policy in airfreight. It is also the reason I would support a more open policy on reducing multimodal barriers. In contrast to our $200 million worth of airfreight purchases, we buy $60 million worth of ocean freight. On the surface, our toughest competition is the multimodal overseas shipping companies, such as Shenker and Kuhn and Nagel, who are able to construct and finance their vessels in an entirely different way. If we go into the future without the flexibility and economies that multimodalism brings, our transportation effectiveness would be reduced nationwide. Our experience shows we are stronger given the flexibility to move in any mode. I think competition from others as a result of deregulation has made us a healthier company than we were five years ago. I believe the same can be true for surface transportation as well.

MR. BARNUM: Clint Whitehurst, who first suggested that AEI hold this seminar, is going to work with us to put together the book of the seminar proceedings. I wanted you to meet Professor Whitehurst, and he may have a comment to put in here.

PROFESSOR WHITEHURST: I have two comments. First, several of the chairmen of the regulatory commissions have made the observation that nobody was beating on their door asking why multimodal companies have not come about. This is quite true, in a general sense, but the idea has been around for a long time. When the proceedings are published, the volume will contain a bibliography with a number of good references arguing for and against multimodal companies. It will be a good place to start learning more about the multimodal concept, and it will refer to some well-reasoned and analytical pieces dealing with multimodal transportation companies.

My second comment is that we must shake out the U.S. transportation system in general. Most of us here realize we have too many firms and too much right-of-way. There are going to be losers—there is no way around it. I strongly suggest that we cannot do anything about this and that we should not. We accept loss in other sectors. We accept companies' going bankrupt. We accept mom and pop grocery stores' going down the tube. But some of the comments that I heard today seemed to infer that in transportation we must protect against loss. Actually, loss is just the other side of the profit coin. In a free market economy we cannot talk about one without the other.

MR. MCLAUGHLIN: John Terry indicated some people were in favor of multimodal ownership because of weakness, and that is not exactly what I said. I don't think our industry as a whole—

MR. TERRY: I did not mean that. I said that the ones that were having more problems seemed to be more interested in freedom.

MR. MCLAUGHLIN: We are more interested in equalization of opportunity than we are in multimodal ownership. As for the railroads' not being able to get a good rate of return, we read this week that Western Pacific Industries is disposing of its railroad property. Who knows, maybe they are doing this so they can buy a truck line.

MR. BROWNE: Perhaps one of the reasons the agencies are not having their door kicked in for intermodal ownership is that when a regulated industry thinks of diversification it wants to get into a nonregulated business to get a better rate of return.

MR. BARNUM: That has been proven by the marketplace.

Thank you all very much for your attention. I join Hays Watkins in thanking Harvey Romoff, Paul Roberts, and Rodney Eyster for preparing the background papers. I was pleased to hear that they were helpful to you.

EPILOGUE

Clinton H. Whitehurst, Jr.

Those who have read the proceedings to this point would probably agree that the conference was comprehensive, balanced, informative, and provocative. If they were not previously aware of the arguments for and against allowing multimodal transportation companies to be formed without restrictions, they are now, if not experts, quite knowledgeable about most of the issues. One interesting question, however, was not on the conference agenda: What is the *likelihood* of legislative and/or administrative barriers to the formation of multimodals being lowered or abolished? Although a major conference issue was whether multimodal firms would be formed if present barriers were removed, the probability of their removal at some time in the future (likely? very likely? never?) was not estimated. In assessing probabilities, however, we must note that decisions, including legislative action and those made by regulatory agencies, are not made in a vacuum independent of real world considerations. Thus, decisions affecting the formation of multimodal transportation companies will in large measure depend upon the present and foreseeable U.S. "transportation environment." This environment has been, and will continue to be, shaped by a number of transportation problems, issues, and trends.

One problem is private sector financing of transportation capital requirements. Exclusive of Conrail and Amtrak needs, it is estimated that $166 billion will be needed by the transportation industry over the next decade. For an industry that is cyclical in nature and with historically low returns on investment, this could be a crucial problem. A recent Department of Transportation study estimated that railroads could face a capital shortfall of as much as $16 billion over the next ten years.[1]

If the private sector will not finance transportation requirements, the only alternative is federal funding.[2] But the temper of the times is to

---

[1] U.S. Department of Transportation, *A Prospectus for Change in the Freight Railroad Industry* (Washington, D.C., 1978).

[2] At present the federal government spends $18 billion annually on transportation programs. This is a humble sum, however, when contrasted to the estimated $330 billion necessary to bring the nation's highway system up to an acceptable level of maintenance.

rein in government spending, not to undertake new projects. Thus, if a convincing case were made that multimodal transportation companies could provide the necessary service and be less dependent on federal support, favorable congressional and regulatory agency action would be more likely. In other words, decision makers would be more willing to accept "losses" by individual interests if the whole could be made healthy.

The trend within government toward deregulation has affected and will continue to affect the environment in which transportation decisions are made. A start was made with passage of the 4R Act of 1976. Neither the railroads, Congress, nor the Department of Transportation is satisfied with the results, however. Further rail deregulation proposals can be expected to get priority attention when the new Congress convenes in January of 1979. In fact, Interstate Commerce Commission Vice Chairman Betty Jo Christian has advised the railroad industry to go to Congress for relief in those instances in which they feel the ICC's interpretation of the 4R Act is restrictive.

An airline deregulation bill already has become law, and truck deregulation advocates in Congress can be expected to press for a deregulation bill in 1979. Thus, with further rail deregulation most likely, some form of truck deregulation likely, and airline deregulation a fact, can the deregulation momentum be stopped or will it carry forward into other areas? In this context, is removing barriers to the formation of multimodal firms not simply a continuation of the deregulation process? Moreover, in assessing the effects of deregulation we cannot ignore the success of the Civil Aeronautics Board's deregulation efforts. In the words of Elizabeth Bailey, a member of the CAB, "less regulation does not spell disaster," and "it is hard to argue any more that we are wild-eyed theorists when the theories we have advocated have led to a year of very substantial profitability for the airlines and very substantially lowered prices for consumers."[3]

Past and present administrations have focused attention on America's energy problem and on transportation, the largest energy user, in particular. Few transportation–energy issues, however, have received as much attention as the fact that energy-efficient piggyback shipments (highway trailers moved on a railroad flatcar) accounted for only 6.9 percent of total railroad carloadings in 1977. While the use of piggyback continues to grow, most observers in industry and government feel that the potential of the system is not being realized. In 1977 the U.S. General Accounting Office issued a report on truck-rail transportation and another on energy conservation by trucks.[4] The energy

---

[3] Remarks of Elizabeth E. Bailey before the Thirty-Third Annual Transportation and Logistics Forum, Washington, D.C., October 3, 1978.
[4] Comptroller General of the United States, *Energy Conservation Competes with*

report detailed the savings possible by greater use of piggyback and recommended that the ICC review its policies and regulations that impede piggyback use. The truck-rail study specifically recommended that the ICC "eliminate or modify restrictions on rail-owned trucking companies so that these railroads can perform piggyback more effectively." [5]

Another part of the transportation environment is the general acceptance that railroads no longer possess OPEC-like power. Passage of the 4R Act in 1976 was a partial recognition of this fact. Further recognition came with the enactment in 1978 of a waterway user tax for the first time. (In the past it was successfully argued that a waterway user tax would drive the barge industry out of business to the ultimate benefit of railroad monopolies.) In addition, the trucking industry has softened its opposition to putting railroads on a more equal footing with other transport modes. With the establishment of a quasi-nationalized Amtrak and Conrail and the open discussion of complete rail nationalization, the trucking industry has recognized its clear interest in seeing that its chief competitor remains in the private sector. As pointed out by John Terry in his remarks, no trucker is anxious to compete with the government. If, however, truckers as well as other modes endorse the concept of more equity with respect to right-of-way costs and the modification of some aspects of restrictive railroad legislation (to allow transcontinental railroads, for example), can they admit the part and not the whole? Is there such a thing as partial equity? If there is no legal prohibition against a motor or water carrier owning a railroad, can barriers to railroads acquiring truck and barge lines be defended? In the broad sense, can prohibitions against horizontal acquisitions in transportation be rationalized when such acquisitions are allowed in other industries subject only to antitrust constraints?

The Consolidated Rail Corporation (Conrail), which inaugurated rail service in 1976 as the successor to the Penn Central and five other bankrupt Northeastern railroads, was not envisioned as a perpetual ward of the federal government. Policy makers foresaw a money-making corporation in place within three years. Updated forecasts, however, offer little hope that this objective is achievable in three years or ever with the present route structure. Already Conrail has used its initial $2.1 billion federal grant and will receive another $1.2 billion. The U.S. Railway Association, which supervises Conrail's financing, estimated as much as $6.5 billion more may be needed to sustain operations through 1988. One alternative to a continued government subsidy for Conrail is nationalization—an anathema to truckers. Another alternative

Regulatory Objectives for Truckers (Washington, D.C.: U.S. General Accounting Office, 1977); and *Combined Truck/Rail Transportation Service: Action Needed to Enhance Effectiveness* (Washington, D.C.: U.S. General Accounting Office, 1977).
[5] *Combined Truck/Rail Transportation Service,* p. 30.

is a severe pruning of the present 17,000 miles of track, perhaps by as much as half. Abandoning unprofitable segments of the system, however, would leave many areas without transportation service. One solution would be to allow Conrail to become a true truck-rail operation, replacing abandoned rail service with trucks and thereby keeping a large part of the system in place. In his remarks, Ben Biaggini noted that just such an option was exercised by Southern Pacific. There is, of course, no guarantee that substituting truck for rail would insure profitability. Nor is there any guarantee that merely paring the present system would create a viable operation. It is clear, however, that something must be done. The choice might well come to nationalization or mandating that Conrail become a multimodal transportation company. If, however, analysis indicates that an extensive substitution of truck for rail service has promise, legislators and the ICC would face a dilemma. Could barriers to forming multimodal companies be dropped for one railroad and not for all?

Airline deregulation is now a fact of life. The Carter administration has made control of inflation its number-one goal and is counting on deregulation in transportation to help achieve it. For better or worse, energy considerations now drive Department of Transportation policies. Financing transportation capital requirements is a continuing industry problem. Conrail service must be cut drastically or the federal government must be prepared to subsidize the system in perpetuity. Railroads no longer possess great economic power. In terms of assets, the largest transportation company, Southern Pacific, would rank only thirty-sixth if fitted into the *Fortune* 500 list, the largest airline only fifty-second, and the largest trucking operation but three hundred twenty-fifth. Exxon, number one, would dwarf the combined assets of the ten largest transportation companies in the United States.

The answer to whether multimodal transportation companies are down the road depends on one's perspective. From the viewpoint of individual transportation interests, it would seem unlikely since, as a number of participants pointed out, no one is kicking down the door to have the barriers removed. Recently, however, events have tended to outrun the decision makers. When that occurs the pressure is on to act. More significant transportation legislation has been passed by Congress in the last two years than in the previous twenty. It is concluded here, therefore, that overall, *and in the context of the total transportation environment,* the probability of multimodal companies in the foreseeable future must be judged as quite high.

APPENDIX
Description of Piggyback Plans

(from ICC Field Service Manual)

Plan I is the movement of motor common carrier freight in the motor carrier's own trailers. The motor carrier is responsible for draying the trailers to and from the railroad ramp. The motor carrier issues a bill of lading to the shipper and pays the railroad an agreed charge based on contractual arrangement for the movement of its trailer. Plan I is actually a substituted rail service. Under Plan I the motor carrier *must* have underlying operating authority.

Plan II is a complete transportation service performed by the rail-road. The railroad, in addition to providing the underlying rail trans-portation on flatcars, furnishes the trailer and provides drayage of the trailer between ramp and facility of shipper or consignee located within the railroad's terminal area. The shipments move on rates published in the rail tariff. Some Plan II rates provide for the loading and/or unloading of trailers by the railroad; however, generally the loading and unloading of trailers is the responsibility of the shipper and/or consignee.

Plan II¼: Railroads quite often have variations of Plan II½, road. It is similar to Plan II except that under Plan II½ drayage of the trailer to and from the rail ramp is the responsibility of the shipper and/or consignee. As a result, rates are lower in Plan II½ than in Plan II.

Plan II¼: Railroads quite often have variations of Plan II½, calling them II¼ or II¾, whereby the railroad states in its tariff that it will provide trailer drayage at *either* origin *or* destination.

Plan III is very similar to Plan II½ in that the railroad provides a ramp-to-ramp service. The difference is that under Plan III the shipper furnishes the trailer. The railroad may lease trailers to shippers; however, the railroad must have a tariff provision with respect to the leases specifying the charges.

Plan IV is the underlying transportation by rail of shipper-owned flatcars and trailers. The predominant users of this plan are freight forwarders and associations of shippers. The railroads may lease flat-cars as well as trailers; however, to do so they must have appropriate tariff publication with specific charges.

Plan V is a truly intermodal service involving a joint motor-rail-motor, rail-motor, motor-rail, or any combination thereof, movement. Rates charged the underlying patron may be rail or motor; however, they are generally motor. The railroads and motor carriers involved have an interchange agreement for movement of the trailer and, in addition, an agreement as to the division of revenue.

BIBLIOGRAPHY

Armitage, K. J. "Integrated Road/Rail Services." *Chartered Institute of Transport Journal* (March 1975), pp. 224-227.

The owner of a British company discusses the successful operation of integrated road/rail service with British Rail. The author stresses the importance of single management control of the integrated operation.

Beardsley, Peter T. "Integrated Ownership of Transportation Companies and the Public Interest." *George Washington Law Review* 31 (October 1962): 85-105.

This article presents supportive arguments for retaining current legislation that bars railroads from unrestricted ownership of other transportation modes. The author concludes that few benefits and many potential dangers, especially for small shippers dependent on public transportation, would result from allowing railroads freedom to enter other modes of transportation.

"Bricks by Freightliner." *Modern Railways* (August 1974), pp. 312-315.

This paper discusses the British Freightliner rail-container service, which was jointly developed by London Brick Company and Freightliners, Ltd.

Buland, George L., and Frederick E. Fuhrman, "Integrated Ownership: The Case for Removing Existing Restrictions on Common Ownership of the Several Forms of Transportation." *George Washington Law Review* 31 (October 1962): 156-185.

This article discusses the economic status of carriers, desirability of transportation coordination, and the present progress of coordination. It concludes that transportation coordination under different ownership is difficult because each mode will seek to gain the greatest return for its share of the haul. Common ownership is believed to be desirable in view of the mature status of each of the transportation modes.

Claytor, W. Graham, Jr. "A Single Intermodal Transportation Company." *Transportation Journal* (Spring 1972), pp. 31-38.

The Southern Railway's chairman (now secretary of the navy) discusses the advantages of intermodal transportation companies and how such companies can be created. Reference is made to the successful multimodal ownership of transportation services in Canada.

Coleman, William T., Jr. *A Statement of National Transportation Policy.* Washington, D.C.: U.S. Government Printing Office, September 17, 1975, pp. 21-22.

The former secretary of transportation discusses intermodal relationships with respect to national transportation policy. He advocates the removal of barriers inhibiting efficient intermodal operations.

Constantin, J. A., R. E. Jerman, and R. D. Anderson. "Rail, Motor and Shipper Opinions on Regulatory Issues." *Transportation Journal* (Fall 1977), p. 49.

A section of this article presents a brief discussion on the formation of transportation companies and the opinions of rail carriers, motor carriers, and shippers concerning possible effects of transportation companies on competition and rates.

Creedy, John A. "Intermodal Ownership and Voluntary Coordination." *Transportation Journal* (Winter 1972), pp. 39-45.

The author presents a case for voluntary coordination of transportation among different modes rather than intermodal ownership. The main arguments against intermodal ownership concern the possibility of railroad domination leading to a monopoly situation and less price competition.

Davis, G. M., M. T. Farris, and J. J. Holder, Jr. *Management of Transportation Carriers.* New York: Praeger Publishers, Inc., 1975, pp. 81-84.

Intermodal ownership is discussed as an interesting alternative to existing policy. Public policy issues involved with intermodal ownership are discussed.

Dillon, Thomas F. "Are Total Transportation Companies Up the Road?" *Purchasing* 81 (November 9, 1976): 68-71.

Some pro and con viewpoints on multimodal transportation companies are presented by executives of transportation companies. The necessity for reforms in transportation regulation and for a national transportation policy is also discussed.

Dodge, William H. "Transportation Pricing Innovation to Promote Economic Efficiency." *ICC Practitioners' Journal* 37 (July-August 1970): 732-745.

The author presents a pricing scheme to foster an economic allocation of traffic under common ownership and to promote transportation coordination.

Douglas, Peter S. "The Economic Irrelevance of Common Ownership." *ICC Practitioners' Journal* 36 (July-August 1969): 1794-1800.

The author questions the economic benefits of common ownership which are frequently claimed by supporters of common ownership. Though he recognizes the need for coordination of U.S. transportation modes, his opinion is that it is economically irrelevant whether this coordination is achieved within the present legal framework or with common ownership.

Elliott, Benton H., and Philip S. Noble. "Intermodal Transportation Systems." *Conference Proceedings: Intersociety Conference on Transportation.* New York: Society of Automotive Engineers, 1972, pp. 40-51.

A history of the development of intermodal transportation systems is presented and current intermodal systems are discussed. It is suggested that transportation companies and the government put emphasis on a systems approach to provide the necessary coordination in intermodal transportation.

Fair, Marvin L., and Ernest W. Williams. *Economics of Transportation and Logistics.* Dallas, Tex.: Business Publications, Inc., 1975, pp. 280-281. The Southern Pacific motor carrier operations and the intermodal operations of Canadian railroads are offered as examples of intermodal management. Advantages and limitations of intermodal managements are discussed.

Fraley, Orrin H. "A Single Intermodal Transportation Company." *Transportation Journal* (Spring 1972), pp. 53-58. The author points out that competition among the various modes of transportation has hindered the development of intermodal transportation. Several intermodal companies are mentioned and the management of one such company is discussed.

Frederick, John H. *Improving National Transportation Policy.* Washington, D.C.: American Enterprise Institute, 1959, pp. 40-42. Two approaches to achieving transportation coordination are presented: common ownership and coordination of modes (that is, through joint agreements among the different modes). It is concluded that common ownership offers more advantages than working agreements among the modes.

"Freightliner Progress." *Modern Railways* (August 1974), pp. 315-318. This article discusses the Freightliner intermodal concept developed in the early 1960s by British Rail which led to the establishment of a new company, Freightliners, Ltd., under the control of state-owned National Freight Corporation, whose main concern is road-haulage operations.

Friedlaender, Ann F. *The Dilemma of Freight Transport Regulation.* Washington, D.C.: Brookings Institution, 1969, pp. 155-159, 166-168, 185-187. Transportation companies are discussed as an alternative to present freight transport policies. The social and economic benefits and limitations of transportation companies are analyzed.

Fulda, Carl H. "Rail-Motor Competition: Motor-Carrier Operations by Railroads." *Northwestern University Law Review* 54 (May-June 1959): 156-209. This article discusses legal cases dealing with rail-motor competition. Analysis of the cases indicates that existing policy with regard to railroad ownership of other modes is desirable to guard against transportation monopoly and to preserve the inherent advantages of each transportation mode.

Gill, L. E. "The Transportation Challenge." *Transportation Journal* (March 1972), pp. 39-45. This paper points out five ways to reach the goal of a coordinated transportation system. Included is the establishment of intermodal companies to cut handling costs and provide an efficient system for dispersal of goods.

Harper, Donald V. *Transportation in America: Users, Carriers, Government.* Englewood Cliffs, N.J.: Prentice-Hall, 1978, pp. 537-553. A chapter of the book deals with government economic regulation and intermodal relationships, including a section on integrated transportation.

Hatchett, R. L. "Implications of the British Freightliner for the Future of American Railroads." *Geographic Perspectives on the Future of Ameri-*

can Railroads, Proceedings of the Special Session of the Annual Meeting of the Association of American Geographics (April 1973), pp. 37-57.

This study discusses containerization and the associated restructuring of operational procedures and freight distribution patterns, focusing on the Freightliner system of Great Britain.

Hazard, John L. *Transportation: Management, Economics, Policy.* Cambridge, Md.: Cornell Maritime Press, 1977, pp. 28-29, 73-74.

The intermodal approach to freight transportation is described. Intermodal ownership is given as one means of coordinating intermodal systems.

Heaver, Trevor D. "Multi-Modal Ownership: The Canadian Experience." *Transportation Journal* (Fall 1971), pp. 14-28.

This article discusses the extent of multimodal ownership in Canada, some general arguments for and against common ownership, the organization and management of a multimodal company, and the impact of management structure on economic benefits.

Helmetag, Carl, Jr. "Common Ownership of Rail and Motor Carriers: The Case for the Railroads." *Texas Law Review* 48, pt. 2 (May 1970): 889-907.

The author refutes arguments that railroads will enjoy unfair competitive advantage under common ownership. He discusses reasons voluntary cooperation among different transportation modes is not successful and concludes that common ownership is the only way to attain coordinated transportation.

Hilton, G. W. *Northeast Railroad Problems.* Washington, D.C.: American Enterprise Institute, 1975.

This monograph examines the sources of the current problems of the bankrupt railroads of the northeastern United States. The author proposes that the railroads be reorganized into a competitive industry of four to seven nationwide integrated transportation companies, using containerized technology for general cargo.

"Is There an Option to the Canal?" *Greenville* [S.C.] *News* (November 14, 1977), p. 4-A.

In this editorial the land-bridge concept is discussed as an alternative to shipping through the Panama Canal. Multimodal transportation firms are deemed desirable in the attainment of an economically efficient land-bridge system.

Janner, A. E. "Canadian Pacific Backs the Container." *Railway Gazette International* (August 1975), pp. 293-295.

The cooperation between modes of transportation in Canada gives Canadians a distinct advantage not only in developing intermodal domestic freight but also as a land bridge for maritime containers moving between the Far East and Europe, as well as to the U.S. Midwest.

Lieb, Robert C. "Intermodal Ownership—A Limited Reality." *Quarterly Review of Economics and Business* (Summer 1971), pp. 71-81.

This article details the participation of various modes of transportation in intermodal ownership as permitted under current regulations. The current level of intermodal ownership differs greatly among the various modes.

———. "Intermodal Ownership: Experience and Evaluation." *ICC Practitioners' Journal* 38 (July-August 1971): 746-759.
The author states several negative propositions concerning intermodal ownership and analyzes the validity of each proposition in view of past experience with intermodal ownership in the United States and Canada and with respect to rational economic behavior. He concludes that many of the arguments against common ownership are not valid.

———. "A Revised Intermodal Ownership Policy." *Transportation Journal* (Summer 1971), pp. 48-53.
The author discusses flaws in current intermodal ownership standards and suggests a revised policy which would permit all forms of transportation integration, subject to the approval of regulatory agencies.

———. *Freight Transportation: A Study of Federal Intermodal Ownership Policy.* New York: Praeger, 1972.
This book is an in-depth study of intermodal ownership, including federal regulation of intermodal ownership with respect to the various transportation modes, a survey of intermodal ownership in the United States, and recommendations for a revised intermodal ownership policy.

———. *Transportation: The Domestic System.* Reston, Va.: Reston Publishing Co., 1978, pp. 326-352.
A chapter is devoted to the discussion of consolidations, intermodal ownership, and conglomerate combinations in transportation.

Locklin, Philip D. *Economics of Transportation.* Homewood, Ill.: Richard D. Irwin, 1975, pp. 860-872.
Common ownership of various combination of transportation modes is discussed, and a history of the regulations prohibiting common ownership is presented. Attention is given to the argument of railroad dominance under common ownership.

Luna, Charles. *The UTU Handbook of Transportation in America.* New York: Popular Library, 1971, pp. 181-183.
Some of the barriers to the formation of transportation companies are discussed. The author warns that transportation companies may pose some disadvantages to shippers, including the loss of consumer-determined choice of transportation mode and possibly a narrow choice of transportation modes.

Margetts, F. C. "Trains for Tomorrow." *Trains* (April 1976), pp. 40-47.
The British Rail's Freightliner combines rail and highway movement of general merchandise in such a way as to maximize the benefits of fast through-train movement, containerization, selected terminal concentration, and modern collection and distribution systems by highway. The author describes this as the only means for a railway in an industrialized country to participate satisfactorily in the movement of freight.

Maritime Transportation Research Board. *Legal Impediments to International Intermodal Transportation: Selected Problems, Options, and Recommended Solutions.* Washington, D.C.: National Academy of Sciences, 1971, pp. 87-88.
A section of the study points out that the conditions which resulted in the

regulations prohibiting common ownership of different transportation modes no longer exist. A recommendation is made for a thorough study of the potential benefits and potential dangers of common ownership.

Melton, Lee J., Jr. "Transportation Coordination and Regulatory Philosophy." *Law and Contemporary Problems* 24 (Autumn 1959): 622-642.

This article discusses the concept of transportation coordination and the various levels of coordination which can exist. It is suggested that transportation companies offer the most satisfactory long-run solution to the problem of transportation coordination.

"Memorandum Concerning Certain Legal Matters in Connection with International Regulation for Combined Transport." *Bulletin des Transports International par Chemin de Fer* (French/German, July 1974), pp. 126-144.

This document was prepared for the United Nations Conference on Trade and Development as part of the groundwork for a Convention for Multimodal International Transport. The document discusses the legal, technical, and economic aspects of international multimodal transport.

Minor, Robert W. "Coordinated or Integrated Transportation." *ICC Practitioners' Journal* 26, pt. 1 (October 1958): 16-31. Remarks at 29th Annual Meeting, Association of Interstate Commerce Commission Practitioners, Washington, D.C., May 8, 1958.

In these remarks the speaker discusses the concepts of transportation coordination (implying cooperation) and integration (implying unification services), and legislation and other issues related to these concepts.

Mott, George Fox, ed. *Transportation Century.* Baton Rouge, La.: Louisiana State University Press, 1966, pp. 187-193.

In a chapter on diversification, the establishment of diversified transportation companies is discussed. Reliance on antitrust laws would provide protection against the possible undesirable consequences cited by opponents of diversified transportation companies.

Norton, Hugh S. *Modern Transportation Economics.* Columbus, Ohio: Charles E. Merrill, 1963, pp. 376-380.

The author discusses policy issues and prospects of transportation integration under single ownership and suggests that common ownership would serve the national interest as well as the interests of the transportation industry.

Nupp, Byran. "Regulatory Standards in Common Ownership in Transportation." *ICC Practitioners' Journal* 34 (November-December 1966): 21-38. This article gives a legislative history of provisions governing common ownership with respect to water carriers, motor carriers, air carriers, and freight forwarders. The author advocates a broader common ownership doctrine and suggests criteria which common ownership applicants might be expected to meet.

"Opportunities in Intermodal Transportation." *Industrial Development* 145 (March 1976): 2-6.

This article emphasizes the importance that intermodal transportation will have to the industrial facility planner. Several concepts of future intermodal transportation centers are illustrated.

Pegrun, Dudley F. *Transportation: Economics and Public Policy.* Home-wood, Ill.: Richard D. Irwin, 1968, pp. 460-466.
A discussion of transportation integration ranges from integration for supplemental purposes to the formation of transportation companies. The author presents some limitations of transportation companies and suggests that supplemental integration may offer advantages in effective coordination over transportation companies.

———. "Restructuring the Transport System." In *The Future of American Transportation,* edited by Ernest W. Williams, Jr. Englewood Cliffs, N.J.: Prentice-Hall, 1971, pp. 74-76.
The author discusses the integrated transportation company as a concept favored primarily by railroads. Some limitations and possible drawbacks are discussed.

Perlman, Alfred E. "The Role of Intermodality." *Defense Transportation Journal* (February 1976), pp. 6-11.
This article discusses the role of intermodality in future transportation systems, with an emphasis on containerization. Common ownership is seen as a necessary condition for the most efficient functioning of an intermodal system.

"Rail Transit Time Reduced by Great Lake Intermodal Service." *Canadian Transportation and Distribution Management* (November 1974), p. 37.
This article discusses the saving in transit time resulting from a new rail car–barge service started by a Canadian company.

"Real Intermodalists See Containers as Profitable, but with Problems." *Containers News* (August 1974), pp. 9-12.
The intermodal service directors of nine railroad lines discuss four major problem areas facing domestic container traffic, including government regulations which limit full utilization of containers and trailers by railroads.

Reebie and Associates, Inc. "Conrail Bi-Modal and Inter-modal Operations: A Study and Plan." National Technical Information Service, 5285 Port Royal Road, Springfield, Va. 22151; PB-239038, DOTL NTIS.
This study discusses the historical development of intermodal operations and identifies economic and organizational problems and opportunities.

Sampson, Roy J., and Martin T. Farris. *Domestic Transportation: Practice, Theory, and Policy.* Boston: Houghton Mifflin, 1966, pp. 311-329.
A chapter of the book covers transportation unification and integration, which are defined as intra- and intermodal common ownership, respectively. Unification and integration are discussed in terms of their methods and purposes, their immediate and long-term effects, the obstacles to them, and public policy.

"Second-generation Freightliner Proposed to Capture Medium-haul Merchandise." *Railway Gazette International* (February 1976).
Improvements on the present British Freightliner system are discussed, including a network of fast container trains linking 300 terminals through sorting centers based on automated warehouse principles.

Stitt, Carolyn Cox. "Common Ownership of Rail and Motor Carriers: The Case against the Railroads." *Texas Law Review* 48, pt. 1 (January 1970): 460-479.

The dangers of railroad domination of motor-carrier operations under common ownership is discussed. The author concludes that transportation coordination can successfully be attained under current legislation, which prohibits railroad entry into other modes.

Sulflow, James E., and Stanley J. Hille. "Transportation Company: An Argument for Intermodal Ownership." *Land Economics* 46 (3) (August 1970): 275-286.

This article illustrates the economic benefits that might be gained through the existence of multimodal transportation companies. Economic and financial analyses are presented, and an economic model of a multiple-product firm is utilized to explain the economics of a transportation company.

"Transportation—The Future." *Proceedings of the Thirteenth Annual Meeting, Transportation Research Forum* 13, no. 1 (November 1972).

Two major challenges face the transportation industry in North America: (1) the impending energy shortage and (2) the integration of different transportation technologies, using the best technology to service a given market on a consistent rational systems approach.

Tripp, Robert S. "A Simulation Analysis of the Economic Consequences of Establishing Multimodal Transportation Companies." Air Force Institute of Technology Technical Report #AFIT-TS-7-6, December 1972. Available from National Technical Information Service, 5285 Port Royal Road, Springfield, Va. 22151; AD-753780, DOTL NTIS.

A simulation study was conducted to help determine whether a transportation company or single modal carriers are economically superior. The factors used in the analysis were: operating ratios of truck and rail modes, the load factors of these modes, the amount of available capacity, and the level of shippers' logistics constraints.

Tripp, Robert S., Norman L. Chervany, and Frederick J. Beier. "An Economic Analysis of the Multi-modal Transportation Company: A Simulation Approach." *Logistics and Transportation Review* 9, no. 1 (1973): 69-84.

This paper presents a methodology for examining the economic consequences of establishing multimodal transportation companies and, using this methodology, compares operations of a multimodal transportation company with the operations of single modal carriers. The results of the study indicate that significant reductions in costs can be realized through the establishment of transportation companies.

"Trucks, Trains, Planes, Boats, All in One Company?" *U.S. News and World Report* (September 25, 1967), pp. 118-120.

This article discusses some of the reasons underlying changes in the attitudes of many transportation industry leaders and government officials toward favoring multimodal transportation companies. Statistics are given which provide some comparisons of the wealth of the largest transportation companies of different modes.

U.S. General Accounting Office. *Combined Truck/Rail Transportation Service: Action Needed to Enhance Effectiveness.* Report to the Congress, December 2, 1977.
In this report piggyback transportation is discussed as a desirable transportation option to increase efficiency and conserve energy. Recommendations to promote the use of piggyback include permitting rail-owned trucking companies.

Welsh, Philip F. "The Right of Railroads to Engage in Water Transportation." *ICC Practitioners' Journal* 24 (1956): 139.
This article discusses railroad control of water carriers under the Panama Canal Act.

Whitehurst, Clinton H., Jr. *The Defense Transportation System: Competitor or Complement to the Private Sector?* Washington, D.C.: American Enterprise Institute, 1976, pp. 109-118.
A chapter on intermodal transportation focuses on problems associated with Department of Defense interfaces with the commercial U.S. intermodal transportation system and suggests that corporate ownership of different transportation modes is only a matter of time.

———. "Managing Defense Transportation: A Proposal." *Translog: The Journal of Military Traffic Management* (April 1977), pp. 2-3, 17-19.
In this article the formation of multimodal transportation companies and the consolidation of transportation regulatory agencies are proposed as the most efficient steps to take in rejuvenating American transportation. The concept is extended into the military system where a single manager for all defense transportation is advocated.

Index of Participants
in the Discussion

SELECTED AEI PUBLICATIONS

The AEI Economist, Herbert Stein, ed., published monthly (one year, $10; single copy, $1)

Reflections of an Economic Policy Maker: Speeches and Congressional Statements, 1969-1978, Arthur F. Burns (485 pp., paper $6.75, cloth $14.75)

Econometric Model Performance in Forecasting and Policy Assessment, W. Allen Spivey and William J. Wrobleski (77 pp., $3.25)

Contemporary Economic Problems 1978, W. Fellner, project director (353 pp., $6.75)

Notes on Stagflation, Howard S. Ellis (23 pp., $1.25)

Swiss Monetary and Exchange Rate Policy in an Inflationary World, Fritz Leutwiler (14 pp., $1.25)

The Secret of Switzerland's Economic Success, Emil Küng (10 pp., $1.25)

Tax Policies in the 1979 Budget, Rudolph G. Penner, ed. (66 pp., $2.75)

Growth of Government in the West, G. Warren Nutter (94 pp., $2.75)

Seminar in Economic Policy with Gerald R. Ford (14 pp., $1.25)

Federal Reserve Policies and Public Disclosure, Richard D. Erb, ed. (108 pp., paper $3.25, cloth $8.75)

Food and Agricultural Policy (250 pp., paper $4.75, cloth $9.75)

AEI ASSOCIATES PROGRAM

The American Enterprise Institute invites your participation in the competition of ideas through its AEI Associates Program. This program has two objectives:

The first is to broaden the distribution of AEI studies, conferences, forums, and reviews, and thereby to extend public familiarity with the issues. AEI Associates receive regular information on AEI research and programs, and they can order publications and cassettes at a savings.

The second objective is to increase the research activity of the American Enterprise Institute and the dissemination of its published materials to policy makers, the academic community, journalists, and others who help shape public attitudes. Your contribution, which in most cases is partly tax deductible, will help ensure that decision makers have the benefit of scholarly research on the practical options to be considered before programs are formulated. The issues studied by AEI include:

- Defense Policy
- Economic Policy
- Energy Policy
- Foreign Policy
- Government Regulation

- Health Policy
- Legal Policy
- Political and Social Processes
- Social Security and Retirement Policy
- Tax Policy

For more information, write to: AMERICAN ENTERPRISE INSTITUTE
1150 Seventeenth Street, N.W., Washington, D.C. 20036

LIBRARY OF DAVIDSON COLLEGE

Books on regular loan may be checked out for **two weeks**. Books must be presented at the Circulation Desk in order to be renewed.

A fine is charged after date due.

Special books are subject to special regulations at the discretion of the library staff.
